T. JAY'S LOG

The Last Voyage
of the *Frisco Felucca II*

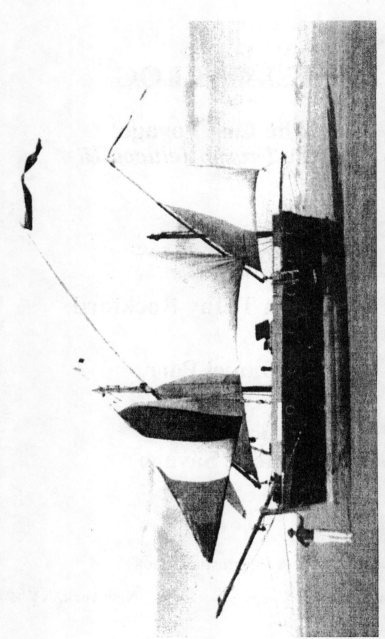

This is a shot of the Frisco Felucca II marooned on Coyote Beach, Mexico.

T. JAY'S LOG

The Last Voyage
of the *Frisco Felucca II*

❦

originally written by

Captain T. Jay Rockford

by

Daniel Parr

❦

drawings by

Hope Savage

A Hearthstone Book

Carlton Press Corp.　　　　　**New York, NY**

This publication was made possible by the generous assistance of
LORD'S INTERNATIONALE INVESTMENTS, INC.,
Palm Beach

Illustrations

Ann von Ramhorst

I've been a sailor all my adult life. Couldn't help it. Ann was a big part of that life, and we lived for years together, always on the water or right next to it. Ann's been gone a few months now and if I'd known she was going to leave so soon, I think I'd probably have tried to sail with her to even more places than we did. Even though I know she's found her ultimate peace and rest, I miss her terribly. She was a wonderful person, and this sixty-four-day log is for her.

I should warn you that I have no regrets. Surely there are things that I "should" have done differently but I didn't do them. I did them the way I did them. And I didn't lie when I wrote them down in the log. Sometimes after I wrote a log entry, something reminded me of something else that was pertinent to things as they were that day, so I wrote that down later. Sometimes it was later the same day; sometimes, later that week, or month. Or whenever. But I didn't lie when I wrote those things, either. I haven't changed the names of the people involved—I see no real need to protect the innocent *or* the guilty—and I didn't write every single day of the voyage.

No matter what, everything's true. It all happened.

Ann understood that the most important thing that happened was not that we got to Hawaii but that we found Paradise somewhere along the way. I hope you'll see that, too. And I hope you'll see how you can become the captain of your own ship, too. Even if it's not a ship like mine, it'll be the ship you need. When that happens, you can take your own voyage that will lead you through the gates of Paradise, too.

The last voyage of the *Frisco Felucca II* was from Puerto Vallarta to Hilo. It lasted sixty-four days. If you get technical about

1

it, the real "last voyage" took far longer than those sixty-four days and was not just across the Pacific to Hawaii. It was a few years. That was the period of time when Ann and I lived aboard the *Felucca* and were always on a voyage to somewhere. This crossing to Hawaii that's logged in here was simply a continuation of a voyage that began well over two years earlier.

But it's those last sixty-four days that are important here. During that time, we broke at least one world's record: we sailed a vessel that steered herself over 3,400 miles across the Pacific. Just establishing that record is enough to please any mariner, and I'm certainly pleased. Too, the editor of *Latitude 38* told me he thought I also broke a second world's record by taking the longest time anyone had ever taken to sail from Mexico to Hilo. I don't think this record matters one way or another even if it's really true. We didn't care how long it took.

We weren't counting the days. Fifty days? So what? We were *enjoying* ourselves! Sixty days? Sixty-four? So what? We enjoyed each dawn, each sunset, middle-of-the-night, each moment we possibly could. Paradise is in the moment, and we had many, many moments when we *knew* we were in Paradise. Yes, it took us sixty-four days to get from Point A to Point B. But we took our home with us. The *Felucca* was our home. And we spent a lot of time in Paradise all along the way.

Today the calendar says I ought to be an old man, but old age is far away for me. I don't have an inkling of what it is. I'm in excellent health, I'm as strong physically as I was at forty, I play my cornet every day, I enjoy eating well, I sleep well—*etc., etc., etc.* After all, I live in Paradise.

Hidden not too deeply in the pages of my log is the story of how I got there. And how I got such fine physical health. And why sixty-four days wasn't long at all.

May 30

I didn't shave this morning. I'm going to grow a moustache. After all, one must do *something* unusual on his first Pacific crossing under sail.

We've been out to sea from Puerto Vallarta for two days on the way to Hawaii. I decided today that it was time to take a serious

2

sighting, and I took the first altitude at 11:00 a.m. Lined up the sun across the compass, slightly north of east. Made a note, using the same compass bearing on the rest of the sights before taking the altitude. Dave Brooks once told me I could get confused unless I took a bearing on the sun early, correcting every sight with that bearing. His prediction has proved true, because yesterday I ignored his suggestion and got nothing accurate. My first fix for longtitude said we were back inside Banderas Bay. Ann laughed when I told her.

But I didn't tell her about this sinking feeling I have in my stomach.

We're lost.

We're only one to two hundred miles off the coast of Mexico, and we're already lost.

Maybe we should turn back? Start over?

No. The Pacific is treacherous and unforgiving, but it's also vast and beautiful. I'm a good sailor. Ann is a good first mate, and this is a safe boat. We'll get there.

Later

David Brooks didn't get there. He was a good sailor in a fine boat, and he had a good first mate, too. He left Puerto Vallarta a few days before we did and he disappeared at sea. Ann and I were the last people to see him alive. Dave was my friend, a fine sculptor and a good sailor, and his disappearance has been hard to accept.

The last time I saw David was in Puerto Vallarta. We'd been there for a couple of months when we were awakened about 2:00 a.m. one morning by a loud male voice. It was shouting my name.

"Rockford, hey, T. Jay Rockford! Are you in there?" The voice sounded familiar, but it was the middle of the night. I had been in a deep sleep and didn't know right away who it was.

"Who is it?" I shouted back.

"It's Dave! David Brooks! Sausalito!"

"I don't believe it!" I shouted. "Come on aboard!"

Dave and a friend came aboard. They had been painting the town red, he said, and had seen my boat. He said he had to come right in to say hello. We were delighted to see each other again,

3

David Brooks' 42-foot racing trimaran,
the Far Horizons

and Ann and I brought out the Ghanga and vino tinto. David, his friend, Ann, and I laughed, talked, reminisced, and had a roaring good time until well after dawn.

The friend was Lou Hayna, a lean robust man who lived in Puerto Vallarta and who had been a German Stuka dive bomber pilot in World War II and who was an unequaled raconteur of war and espionage stories. For several days and nights, the four of us became a familiar sight around Puerto Vallarta and in the sailing community as we partied and enjoyed each other's company. I introduced Dave and Lou to several people who helped us party throughout that beautiful and famous vacation spa, and he and Lou introduced Ann and me to several others. We had a grand good time. (I use "party" as in the sailor's definition: "entertaining aboard one's boat and in related environs, exchanging sea stories, adventures and schemes; and the enjoyable reciprocation of doing the same on other cruising boats, while not working and keeping one's own vessel shipshape.")

David was strikingly energetic, always enthusiastic about living and always involved in something that kept him physically active in some speedy way. Although he wasn't a large man, his 5'10" frame carried a handsome and intriguing look. His bearing and his appearance gave the impression of an excited man who had either just returned from an adventure or was about to embark upon a new one. He had yellow-green eyes, curly dark brown hair and a safari moustache over a clean-shaven, square jaw. Even the shape of his face reminded me of Jack London. He liked to wear a flowered loose shirt, when he wore a shirt, and he frequently wore a Panama hat with seashell band pulled low over his always expressive and bright eyes. He kept a small gold fish-shaped earring in one pierced earlobe; "Pisces," he'd say when people asked him why.

Twelve years earlier, I had watched David build his unusually attractive, angular two-story houseboat on a huge float in the water at Sausalito. From the second floor of the Spreckles House where I lived at the time, before I moved onto the water, I had a view that overlooked ninety percent of that once-hallowed area where the "turned-on" floating people of Sausalito lived, anchored out in the Bay. Each new houseboat was the beginning of an artistic creation; each finished houseboat was a mirror of the builder-artist's very self. Dave's houseboat was truly a remarkably beautiful work of art. It was featured in a photograph in Charles Borden's book *Sea Quest* (p. 81), with a caption beneath that reads:

> "Only step out of my sunlight," said Diogenes. An audacious mid-sixties houseboat from Sausalito designed for ample sunlight and getting away from it all.

David loved to sail. He sold his beautiful houseboat not too long after he finished it, and he used the sale monies to buy a 42-foot racing trimaran, the *Far Horizons*, and sailed it with a sloop, one-mast rigging. It seemed like he was always sailing, always going somewhere or getting back. Three times in a row, his sailing trips were directly to the Hawaiian Islands, and during one of those visits he won an eighty-boat race. A number of trimarans as well as single-hulled vessels were in the race. When David and his three crew members pulled into the Honolulu yacht harbor and dropped the "hook," they dove over the side, swam to the clubhouse, went in, and celebrated their victory with round after round of drinks. No one inside believed Dave when he said that the *Far Horizons* had won the race because no other boats were in sight at first. Finally, when the other racers began to trail in, they confirmed that Dave's vessel had outstripped them all by an enormous margin.

When Ann and I got the news about his disappearance the other day, we were grief-stricken. The trimaran had been found floating upside down. It was totally intact with no visible damage except that her mast, shrouds, and stays were completely missing. The mast and all attachments were cleanly removed, as if by the hands of some giant vandal. Inside the cabin were found the bodies of David's pet monkey and dog. The monkey had survived longer than the dog, because it had eaten much of the dog's carcass before it died. The state of the monkey's body and the barnacles on the wrecked trimaran made it clear that the vessel had been upside down for 60 to 90 days. That's a long time to be lost at sea. Strangely, only the ship-to-shore inflatable skiff, sextant, and compass were gone. David's nephew (and first mate) Bob was gone, too.

6

The sea can be exhilarating and exciting. It can also be unforgiving and cruel. Even the best mariners, like David, can be overcome by the sea. He didn't make it to Hilo. But we will.

May 31

Last night there was no wind. The ship's yards were slatting and banging, making the *Felucca* moan and groan. The sound of wood creaking against wood and the squeak of new rope was hard on my nerves, so I pulled the sails and yards on deck and went uncomfortably to bed. Many vessels roll and pitch and slam and bang in a calm, and ours is no different. I slept fitfully and was awakened at 3:00 in the morning by a breeze that stopped the turmoil. On deck, though, the mess of sails, ropes, and loose ends discouraged any work, so I decided to get some more sleep and tend to the mess at sunup. At dawn there was still a slight wind and I cleared the decks today, leaving nothing superfluous on deck.

The temporary seizing I put at the top of the mainmast needs replacing. I made a new clutch out of ¾-inch Mexican line (the clutch, or *parrel*, is the heavy rope which holds the yard to the mast). With the bosun's chair and Ann's help I got to the top of the mast and rove on the new rope. The detail on deck appears fascinatingly different from up there. And as the boat erratically rolled back and forth in the calm but rumpled sea, I soared in a wide arc back and forth around the mast and thought, "If this line breaks, I'll be *killed*." But my confidence soared as I got the new topping lift in place.

As I worked, I thought how convenient it would be to have a good engine. Instead of sleeping with such difficulty last night in the creaking and rolling ship, I could have just turned on a 25-horse diesel and proceeded westward without losing any momentum. The "modern-day sailor" has this luxury, after all. The modern sailor has a professionally well-built boat with reliable engine, doesn't he? But such a combination does only one thing: it removes the adventure from "sailing across the ocean blue." If a man has to have an engine with his sails, if he has to have this double safeguard against the perils of the sea, he cannot call himself a true "sailing sailor." I still feel that fear in my belly, but, nope, I don't want an engine.

Later

I've had a prejudice against an engine on a sailboat for a long time. I didn't take that anti-engine stance, however, about an engine here on the *Felucca*. At least, not to start with. It was an unplanned event the morning several months ago that we left on this leg of the voyage out into the open sea that "disposed" of our engine. The weatherman had said dawn would crack that morning over San Francisco Bay at precisely 5:45 a.m., and both Ann and I were ready and eager to cast off the very instant our clock read 5:45. We were actually starting our sail to Mexico or Hawaii or wherever—we were sure we were planning to go, at least, to Mexico; Hawaii as a destination came later. Only one thing was certain: we were actually leaving home and getting underway on Our Trip, the voyage most people had told us was impossible. We were ready to keep our oft-repeated pledge "to sail at dawn." I could actually hear my heart thumping with excitement as I pulled up the anchor.

Secretly, I realized we were in a no-win situation, a point-of-no-return. Ann and I had painted ourselves into a tight little corner by announcing so many planned details of Our Trip; it had started out as a leisurely shakedown cruise around the Delta country and now it had grown into a trip to Mexico. Many people had told us our boat wouldn't make it out of San Francisco Bay, but I didn't believe them.

We'd said all of the good-byes we could, and now we couldn't *not* go. The only place left for us to go next was out to the Pacific Ocean through the Golden Gate. The majestic bridge that frames the Gate also framed a special picture for us that morning. I felt the picture was calling out to us, calling for our magical entry into it aboard the *Frisco Felucca II*.

There was very little wind, but it was pushing from the best direction possible, from the east. And the ebbing tide was at its best for us. I spoke aloud to Ann, trying to sound as confident as I could: "I think I'll start the engine. We've got a good wind and good tide, but the engine will help us get offshore before any heavy weather can find us."

Ann knew perfectly well my aversion to engines in general, so she gave me a funny look as I went below with such good cheer to start our engine. It was not the kind of sea or weather where we needed it at that moment. My real reason for wanting to start it up was simply to try it out. I hadn't started this engine since I'd installed it. I'd had it running on a work table at the Uptown Yacht Harbor in Stockton weeks ago, and it ran fine at the time. It was a four-cylinder Star marine gasoline model that looked greasy enough to work, and my disdain for engines on a sailing vessel helped keep me from checking out engine and gear box any sooner. That was near the bottom of my list of priorities.

But it was finally the time, I thought, to see if the engine and home-rigged gear box would put up or shut up. After all, we were actually underway on Our Trip and everybody had told me we couldn't possibly go without an engine, "For heaven's sake!" It was primarily because of all those comments that I installed the damned thing in the first place. The engine started on the first try, but I couldn't get the gears to engage until I slapped them with a hammer a few times. The gears fell into place somehow, the engine puttered loudly, the fair weather sails billowed beautifully, and the world's most beautiful bridge was gliding majestically overhead. Mexico is just a few weeks away!

We watched "Mile Light" pass on our left with the Farallon Island light blinking on and off. Ann and I smiled triumphantly at each other. Whatever lay ahead, we had agreed, would be something we would face *together* and face *lovingly*.

Suddenly, I smelled smoke. Rushing below, I was shocked and flabbergasted to see flames in the after part of the engine room. *"Fire!"* I called frantically—to no one in particular. And fire it was. I could see through the dense smoke that the fire was coming directly from the gear box, fueled to a hot flame by a thick spray of oil that was supposed to wash over the gears. I couldn't find the fire extinguisher quickly, so I grabbed a large Turkish towel and rammed it into the port-side well, trying to soak it with sea water (both wells had sea water in them up to about eight inches from the top; I hadn't yet sealed them with the water baffles). I yanked the dripping wet towel from the well and flung it over

9

hot charcoal, but the fire seemed to go out. The smoke changed from black to a sickly white.

But the fire didn't stay out. I took the towel away to inspect the damage and the fire ignited again with a loud *WHOOSH!* Practically blinded by the new wave of thick, oily smoke that totally blackened everything it touched—including me—I desperately pushed the towel back into the well and slung it again, dripping with seawater, back over the gear box. This time, I left the towel there while I poked my head topside to gasp some fresh air.

Ann looked at my black face with a mixture of horror and gleeful amusement. She seemed not to know whether to laugh out loud or cry out in alarm. I tried to smile and said limply, "Just a little fire in the gear box." As I retreated quickly to tend to whatever I could tend to, I heard Ann laugh out loud. I shouted up to her, "I've got it out now," and this time I know I heard her laughter.

I cleaned up the mess as much as I could. Somehow I'd thought that Ann had stowed the fire extinguisher and I found out later she'd thought I had stowed it. We actually got underway not having one on board. Either way, it was my neglect in checking over all necessary supplies that caused the serious problem of not having a fire extinguisher. There are very good reasons that marine law and common sense require a fire extinguisher on board, and our brief but spectacular fire impressed those reasons on me so severely that I've vowed never to be without one again. And too, the Coast Guard justifiably issues a citation that can be quite costly when it finds a vessel without a fire extinguisher aboard. The fire had ruined the connections between the engine and the gear box, and the engine had lost its connections to spark and fuel. The whole system was now obviously useless so far as I was concerned. There was nothing left to do when I went back topside except to say to Ann, as nonchalantly as I could, "I think we should agree to make this trip without an engine. There's enough wind. We won't use the engine. Who needs it?"

We needed an engine! I realized that it might be foolish not to turn back right then and there. After all, we were still within two miles from the Golden Gate and could very well sail back to San Francisco or Sausalito on the next flood tide and get the engine—and gear box, of course—repaired and properly installed.

We weren't out an hour and already we'd lost the engine! We really shouldn't even be out here on this side of the Golden Gate without an engine! I tried hard to project confidence for Ann's benefit, but I was beginning to think we should turn back.

What would be our explanation to all those people who had just seen us leave? To all those people who had been telling us we shouldn't have left in the first place? To those who doubted us? Who warned us? I was too ashamed to reverse course at once, to turn back and get the engine repaired. I was smarting too much from all those barbs—kindly thrown, mostly, but thrown nonetheless—that said clearly that we could not do what we knew we could do. It was Ann whose calm manner and steady confidence convinced me to keep going. She looked at my frown, wiped some black soot off my face where I'd missed washing it, smiled broadly and said, "We're really underway, aren't we."

That did it. We didn't turn back. We waved good-bye to the Golden Gate and headed down the coast towards Mexico. We left San Francisco without an engine and, even though our choice was sort of involuntary and downright scary when I stopped to think about it, we knew we had started the adventure of a lifetime. Win or lose, we couldn't stop now. We never did repair or replace the engine. We learned a great deal about how to be better sailors because of the accident that took our engine; we haven't had an engine since that gloriously beautiful morning when we left the Golden Gate. And even though there have been a few moments when I've desperately wanted an engine on this voyage, we've done just fine without one. We crossed the Pacific from Mexico to Hawaii without an engine, didn't we?

June 1

It's 3:30 in the afternoon. The wind is blowing about 15 mph, hitting just forward of the beam. The rumpled sea has short distances between swells. Two jibs are flying, along with the lateen-rigged main and mizzen. The *Felucca* is driving along at right angles to the wind—sailing beam wind across the ocean. How nice for her to steer herself with the helm lashed!

I'm dictating this log entry to Ann while reclining on the port side settee below the central cabin as the boat plows through the

11

seas with comfortable motions in spite of the wind velocity and bumpy swells. As soon as the weather improves to a point where I can get a good sight, I'll have some figures on our daily runs. If the rigging and sails hold up, we should make a reasonably fast cruise. What will it take? Ten days? Two weeks at the most?

Shall I lower the smart new mainsail that is drawing so well along with the jib and mizzen? I don't want to take it down. I want to know what the boat can do with a full set of working sails in a 35 mph wind. The wind's picking up and she's lunging harder, leaning about 15 degrees; as a rule she sails closer to vertically straight.

I went on deck to see how my homemade rudder is working. With helm and rudder amidships, there's almost no strain on it. I feel secure because I feel confident that the *Felucca* will steer herself across the Pacific, all the way to Hilo. My only concern is that the wind will increase after dark and I'll have to lower the main by feel alone. I dislike taking the mainsail down at night, so I'll make this decision at sunset.

Ann and I played gin rummy from 4:00 p.m. until now, almost suppertime. I won! . . . and Ann's a genius! It's a thrill to win at gin rummy against Ann; she never "lets me win," and she's such a sharp, good player. How one woman can be so good at so many things constantly amazes me. And lovely. She's one of the loveliest women I've ever known. I'm a lucky man because she's chosen me.

Later

I met my future first mate, Ann von Ramhorst, in a pub on the San Francisco waterfront in the famous old jazz joint, Pier 23, where musicians such as Burt Bales, Robin Hodes, and Bill Napier played "Frisco-style" traditional jazz. It was a Sunday afternoon, and I had sailed to San Francisco's Pier 23 from Sausalito in my 22-foot single-mast lateen rigged steel lifeboat. I dropped anchor opposite the club and climbed the ladder to the dock as patrons in the club gazed at my boat and me in what I took to be wonderment. One of the greatest traditional jazz clarinetists on the West Coast, Bill Napier, and a group were playing "Bill Bailey, Won't You Please Come Home?" as I strolled in.

I remember thinking, "What a beautiful woman!" as I sat down next to her at the bar. We started talking and I found she was there for the same reason I was: to hear some of the best traditional jazz available in San Francisco. Our conversation took over, and I've forgotten most of the details about the music. We talked for hours, and when the band played "Tiger Rag," its last number, lovely Ann invited me to her apartment for dinner and to continue our talk.

She had a charming flat on the 19th floor of a building on Nob Hill, and she lost no time at all in preparing what became a "late supper." By the time we were enjoying eggs Benedict, champagne, and fresh strawberries, I knew she was for me. She was childless and divorced; I was divorced with one child. We made love that night, and we entered a dream world that both of us had always sought. Our Trip really began that night.

We grew closer in the following weeks and months and came to the conclusion that we were both living on the proverbial treadmill that has no end. I was forty-five-years old, not in very good physical shape, and almost totally disenchanted with the way things were in my life. My job as an independent salesman brought in just barely enough to exist, and my oyster that I knew the world to be was continually just out of my reach. Ann was a highly successful executive secretary for a Financial District big bank, earning just barely enough to pay for her rent and food, and she, too, was disenchanted with the world. We were kindred souls, and we were aware of the profound pleasure of finding each other.

We both had dreams of sailing all over the world, of leaving the world of 9-to-5 schedules and problems, of living for ourselves without owing anybody anything, and I came to know that Ann would be the best possible companion for me if I was finally to go after that oyster. Her abilities were so unusual and varied, and she was so skilled as an excellent clothes designer and seamstress, as a gourmet cook (*Sunset Magazine* published seven of her original recipes), as a pastel artist, and other things that were so wonderful to me. She played the piano, the snare drums and high hat, she composed haiku poems, and she was my unofficial psychotherapist and my official partner in every endeavor. I found a truly perfect "first mate."

Soon enough, we pooled our resources and living efforts. And we decided together to change my simple black-hulled houseboat into a moving, lively sailing cruiser that would be our home. It's been our home ever since.

June 2

We were enjoying our cocktail before dinner when a sudden banging sent me scurrying to the topdeck. The clutch on the main yard had broken! Fortunately, I had a second clutch attached to reduce movement and sound, and it held the yard after it had dropped about two feet down the mast. I lowered the sail and rove on a new one from fresh Mexican hemp rope. While I did this repair, we continued sailing under the jib and mizzen.

I was ready to raise the mainsail when I heard another snap, thump, and bang. The stainless steel cable that pulls the rudder back and forth had parted! We're now in a confused sea without a rudder, and the wind's blowing about 15 mph from the northwest. I lowered the jib, leaving the mizzen flying, to head the bow of the ship into the oncoming sea. Without rudder control, we can go nowhere until I adjust the sails for self-steering. Under the mizzen, the *Felucca* points about 45 degrees into the ocean swells. That's safe but uncomfortable. The nights out here get too dark for me to go over the side, so the rudder cable repair will have to wait till daylight.

The difference between moving under full sail and being "hove to" under a mizzen is the difference between night and day, but what else to do without use of the rudder? Ann and I discussed what to do and found no real need to worry. We'd found in cruising in the Delta that the boat will sail herself in a beam wind with the helm lashed amidships. In fact, there's a beam area of 35 degrees or so where we don't need a rudder at all in that kind of wind. So a light flashed on in my mind. There is a beam wind, so we can sail southeast and not worry about the rudder. I went ahead and raised the mainsail. Though our rudder cable was uncontrollable, it trailed along in a midship's position.

So I hoisted the main and watched in disbelief as the ship veered broadside into the wind by herself. It was as if there were a rudder guiding her! In a few brief moments the single mainsail was full, and the boat headed to the left, moving forward confidently and falling off until she was sailing at almost a right angle to the wind! The useless rudder was weaving slightly back and forth at near midship's position, following its leader—the lateen mainsail.

I was so excited that I shouted out loud, "Ann, if I send this story to a yachting magazine, they'd call me a liar!"

I believe we can actually sail all the way to Hawaii without a rudder. If I had realized the *Felucca* would steer herself with no rudder whatsoever on certain points of a good wind, we wouldn't have had to get that tow into Monterey when our first rudder was sheared off. But now that we're under way, the boat rides easily and I'm going to bed early. I need the rest.

While we were still sailing triumphantly without a rudder tonight, two ships appeared on the horizon. I shined a flashlight on the sail, blew my foghorn, played the SOS message on my cornet and finally let loose with "The Twelfth Street Rag." They must have seen or heard something because they both passed us with precious little room to spare; I certainly couldn't have avoided either of them. No rudder, sir.

Later

I'm not all that bothered about sailing without a rudder because of our experiences several days earlier near Monterey. We hadn't planned to stop at Monterey that day we left Sausalito. After the engine fire, we sort of thought nothing else could happen and that we'd stop next somewhere in Mexico. We were in high spirits, though, in spite of having lost our engine, even when we found ourselves in a midday calm about five miles off the Cliff House, rolling, backing, and slamming while actually going nowhere. It was a little bothersome to be becalmed so close to home port, but even a calm sea couldn't calm our enthusiasm at this point.

In late afternoon the wind came up from the west, rather suddenly, and we were off again, slicing through the waves. We estimated our speed at about five miles per hour, and we continued through the night. We took turns at the wheel and by sunrise we were nearing Monterey. "This is a snap," I thought, and Ann and I talked about how well the *Felucca* was sailing, about how beautiful the weather was, and what a short time it would take to reach Mexico.

The wind freshened to a force five and then to a force seven in just a couple of hours. A force seven wind has a velocity that sets whole trees in motion on land and causes difficulty in walking against it. We began reducing sail, putting down the mainsail, replacing it with the storm sail on the mainmast and a small jib forward. I wanted desperately to get past the Point Sur light that is south of Monterey before hoving to because it is at the point where the coast takes a definite turn to the left, throwing sailors completely clear of land. But now we were at a place where we could plainly see the Point Sur light, and the wind just wasn't cooperating. As if it read my intentions and wanted to thwart them, the wind swelled to a steady force eight (on land, this wind would be breaking twigs off trees). The *Felucca* began to show some difficulty in handling. My steering apparatus had too much play in it and the boat wanted to steer herself and broach to when we raced down the face of each overtaking wave. By this time, I'd lost a concept of how fast we were going; it seemed like we were almost about to leave the water and actually fly. She was no longer simply breaking the waves; she was throwing white water off her bow in a continuous roar. With awe in her voice, Ann called the waves "moving whitecapped mountains!" The *Felucca* tried, time after time, to broach to, to turn sideways to the oncoming waves and, most likely, capsize and roll. We marvelled how she kept her deck dry even as she was being slammed broadside by the vigorous sea.

We'd worked up so much speed careening and yawing through those tremendous waves as we were running directly before the gale that I decided to try to slow us down by throwing my triangular wooden sea anchor over the stern. A sea anchor's purpose is to hold the boat's stern directly into the wind, slowing her forward progress and giving her pilot a chance for better control. We began to slow, alright, but our rudder didn't hold up to the beating of the overtaking waves. It gave way completely!

This was disturbing. Downright scary! Our rudder was broken and unusable and there didn't seem to be any chance of even a temporary repair out there so far from land. I sent Ann below at once, telling her that we couldn't sail at all without a rudder. We'd cleared Point Sur and weren't in danger of being thrown against the coast, at least not at this point, not with the current and high wind driving us due south. I put up a jib forward to keep the pointed stern of the boat into the wind so that it would keep blowing us away from the shore. My friend Captain Sam Anderson had recommended I use a wooden sea anchor, made of 1-inch plywood instead of the more usual cloth material. He said skippers of fishing boats prefer wooden ones because they are sturdier and less likely to break. He was right; my homemade wooden sea anchor worked very well and kept us hove to, more or less "anchored" in the same general area.

A sea anchor is a marvelous thing. It will slow and almost stop a vessel. It isn't really an anchor because it doesn't touch bottom but flies like a kite on a chain bridle. As it flies underwater with current acting as its air flow, it works as a drag and thereby hangs a vessel against itself. With a sea anchor out for a twelve-hour shift, a vessel might drift five miles or so rather than the twenty-five it would be likely to drift without one, and the direction of the boat's drift is then determined primarily by the wind and current. The sea anchor also holds a vessel right at 45 degrees from the prevailing wind so that she rides up and over each oncoming wave, avoiding the catastrophe of broaching to and being swamped by the waves.

With the sea anchor out to secure us against broaching to, I went below to join Ann. She had concocted a delicious hot soup for dinner, and we ate heartily while we listened to the heavy seas slamming us constantly. This uncomfortable, raucous heaving continued all night and at times the waves sounded like clumsy, noisy intruders as they pounded the *Felucca*.

The next morning brought some abatement from the gale and a brilliant sun in a cloudless sky. I started early, trying to rig something to work as a rudder for us so that we could get into a port for repairs, but my efforts produced no workable results. I managed to keep us more or less on course by maneuvering the lateen sails; this let us take maximum advantage of existing wind and current in order to stay on a port tack and get closer to the coast. But the night's gale had driven us about twenty-five miles off the coast and about twenty-five miles south of Point Sur, California. We had plenty of sea room and a strong breeze, but we did not have a working rudder.

Incidentally, when we were just a few miles out from the Golden Gate, Herb the Air Force pilot dropped by and kept his word. I heard him first and looked for the noise. There he was: flying his

United States Air Force fighter jet directly at us and what looked like about twenty feet above the water! At the last possible moment, he veered upwards at a 45-degree angle and rolled the plane over and over in a corkscrew fashion. As he flew away from us, he yawed three times—a beautiful maneuver! We'd met Herb only a few days before we left Sausalito and, true to his words, he gave us his grand farewell gesture. As Ann and I watched that jet airplane disappear in the distance, we marveled over the wonder of what Herb had done to wish us well.

That was the day that we lost our beautiful skiff. In the afternoon, the wind continued to grow, picking up to a force five and then to a force six (a wind that will put large branches in motion on land and cause umbrellas to be used with difficulty). We were sailing along beautifully with the skiff on a 50-foot line when she broached to in the waves, filled with water and turned turtle. We couldn't turn back to rescue her with such a terrific sea running; white crests and wind streaks were in the water all around us. Because of the tremendous drag the line finally broke. She was lost. It was quite upsetting to watch her go through the sinking, and when she broke free, Ann burst into tears and we said a sad farewell to the little boat that had taken us to so many wonderful places in the past year.

I was weighing the possibilities of getting all the way to Mexico without a rudder when Ann spotted a ship coming from the south. "We need a tow," she said, laconically. Her manner was an obvious request to me that we should hail the ship and ask for a tow.

It is a humiliating experience for any sailor to accept a tow, but the winds took my pride as quickly as they'd taken my rudder. I "cooperated." Ann immediately found instructions in a sailing book about what to do to send a distress signal, and within twenty minutes produced a white sheet with a big red "X" sewn across the middle. The mizzen was clear of sails, so I used it to hoist our distress signal flag. I lowered all the other sails to help sharpen our image of trouble. Ann stood by the mainmast, a strikingly beautiful woman in distress. I thought that she would be all the signal we ought to need, standing there in her tiny, two-piece bathing suit. But for good measure, she waved a long piece of bright red cloth. I soaked a rag in kerosene and oil, put it in a tin bucket and lit a fire to send huge clouds of black smoke billowing into the air. We took turns using our foghorn to blow the

SOS signal. I even used my cornet to repeat the SOS with a jazz beat, but nothing worked. About the only thing else for us to do would have been to climb the mainmast naked and shoot flares directly at the passing ship.

Happily, we didn't have to make those last efforts. The ship changed course to head towards the *Felucca* and slowly began crossing the two miles that separated us. Her name was the *Enco Gloucester* and her skipper was a real gentleman. When he was near enough, he called over his bullhorn from her flybridge, "What can we do for you?"

"We've lost our rudder and need assistance," I shouted back.

He waved his acknowledgement and veered off, making a large circle in the area around the *Felucca*. Fifteen minutes later, he was close enough again to bellow to us, "The Coast Guard has been notified. They're on their way. Good luck!" And the tanker resumed her course northward. We had never before appreciated help at sea so much.

It would take the Coast Guard several hours to reach us because we were at least fifty miles south of Monterey, well out of sight of land. The *Felucca* was riding easily in the moderate seas, and I put up the jib and mizzen sails to steady her. She stayed with the wind and veered back and forth from one tack to another, more or less keeping her course southward. It was pleasant enough, however, because we knew help was on the way.

Four hours later a Coast Guard cutter arrived. The crew threw us a line and requested that we leave the sea anchor dragging because it would help keep the boat lined up directly behind and help the two go more easily. When all seemed secure, the cutter started the tow.

The tow started with a lurch, followed by a lull followed by a thump. And then we were off at high speed! We were taking waves almost over the bow of the *Felucca* immediately, waves of a size that hadn't come close to washing over the deck even in the gale force winds of the previous day and night. But at this speed, obviously, the tow was much too fast for the *Felucca*.

Frantically, I blasted our foghorn and cornet and made up and down motions with my arms. I was trying to get the Coast Guard's skipper to slow the cutter's speed. I went to the bow and did the same thing. Nobody saw me but Ann. She started waving, too. We must have made quite a sight, jumping up and down, yelling

"Slow down!" in many different ways, blowing SOS on our foghorn and my cornet in the middle of a beautiful day. But nothing worked. The Coast Guard roared on, oblivious to our presence or absence.

We were taking on water in serious ways. At the bow, some of the woodwork sprung, letting water inside. As we watched, the intake grew at an alarming rate and then we found ourselves bailing for our lives! When I thought we were a little ahead of the incoming water, one of us would go on deck to jump up and down again, to blow the foghorn again, to do anything we could think of to get them to slow down, but they just kept going. Ann and I were stunned to realize that we might not survive this life-saving mission!

After about three hours of this desperate effort, the cutter slowed enough so that the water ceased surging over the bow and into the boat. We could relax our bailing. We were exhausted after three hours of being towed. We flopped on the bunk with some hot coffee just in time to notice a change in the rhythmic, regular motion of the towed *Felucca*. I went on deck and, to my utter amazement, found that the 2 ½-inch hawser line had chaffed through. We were adrift again and the Coast Guard was merrily motoring on. I yelled, I blew the foghorn, I even played "Black and Blue" on my cornet.

But there was no reaction from the cutter as it slowly moved away from us, out of sight.

It was the middle of the night before they came back. That particular Coast Guard vessel has a standard crew of six people, and it's clear not one of them on that vessel had watched their tow at any time. They had gone all the way back to Monterey before discovering we weren't trailing along behind them. We were drifting two miles off the Carmel rocks when their search lights found us. They tied us up again for a tow and, while they were close enough to hear, I begged them to tow at a slower pace and please to watch and see that we were still behind them as they went in. A male voice boomed out in the night, telling us that they "couldn't go slower than six knots," so we just had to sit tight and hope for the best. Our boat was soaked from stem to stern with water we'd taken in during the first tow, so it didn't seem to make much difference if we got any more or not. Our wall-to-wall carpets were squishy and sodden with seawater, and

20

our bilges were overflowing into the cabin. The forward part of the boat was damaged by the tow, and Ann and I both were physically and emotionally exhausted. My immediate reaction to the news about the six-knot minimum was, "Well, who cares."

When I get back to United States waters, I'm going to check out that "minimum-speed for towing" business. I've known Coast Guard people from all over; I've seen their dedication at work and have admired their skill and compassion in all kinds of seas. I was and still am genuinely thankful that the Coast Guard towed us in that night. But I've often wondered how in the hell that skipper explained back in Monterey that the distressed boat he was towing in that afternoon had disappeared. What did he say? That he had forgotten it somewhere? It was a profound relief to anchor safely, in the wee hours of the morning, in Monterey Bay, thanks to the United States Coast Guard.

So there we were. Our third morning at sea found us at Monterey for the second time, still without an engine but at anchor this time. This time we had no rudder, a damaged bow, and a soaked boat. But this was Our Trip, and not even the first two days' challenges overwhelmed the magnificence of what we were doing. Our experiences so far had not dampened our enthusiasm or determination one bit.

We rested for two days, pretty much staying below to recover our strength and to clean up the boat. At one point, we noticed Sea Scouts circling us with apparent curiosity about the *Felucca*. I invited them aboard where we found them filled with questions about this boat they'd seen only in pictures before this moment. They were a high-spirited, sharp-minded group of students, and they offered us a ride ashore. We accepted, and they took us to the Monterey Peninsula Yacht Club where some Club members magnanimously offered us use of a skiff until we found one for our own.

We cleaned ourselves and some clothes at the Yacht Club and went off to explore on foot. Right away, we discovered a restaurant that was obviously very popular, and we enjoyed hearing our favorite New Orleans jazz played by a wonderful band. We love that two-beat music with the accent on the second and fourth beats (or the "after beat"), and we were very favorably impressed that the band had a quite traditional composition: cornet, trombone and clarinet for the wind instruments; drums, banjo, and bass for the rhythm and bass line. The sprightly, traditional tunes they played were old standards or, rather, those that were popular from about the 1920s to the 1940s. They played such tunes as "Sweet Georgia Brown," "Ain't Misbehavin'," "When You're Smilin'," "Tin Roof Blues," and many others. The Sea Scouts were too young to join us at the restaurant, and I've often thought that they would have greatly liked that particular kind of music if they had had the chance to hear it just that once.

We enjoyed a pleasant, brief interlude to our voyage during the few days we spent in Monterey. We got a fine skiff—at least as good as the one we'd lost—from Mickey Iverson, a man whose boat was moored alongside the *Felucca*. That deal led to the development of new friendships with the Iversons, a wonderful Thanksgiving dinner at their house, and, later, visits by them with us aboard the *Felucca*. Al Martin performed magic with his welding equipment, and in a short time we produced sturdy and solid new pintles and gudgeons to hold the repaired rudder to the boat. Everything looked as if it would take whatever the Pacific wanted to throw at us. Our stay was only temporary, of course, and with all necessary repairs and equipment taken care of, we were soon ready to be on our way again.

June 3

At 4:00 A.M., I was able to get a sight of Polaris (the North Star) with some accuracy. That star doesn't show brightly in the sky in this 19-degree latitude—the same latitude as Hawaii—so I'm patting myself on the back for even finding it. At dawn I immediately started the cable repair, going over the side into the water; kept a wary eye open for sharks. I hate sharks. Within two hours, the cable was back into A-1 operating condition. We're under full sail again now, about midday. I'm not steering her, though; she's still steering herself. I don't know of any other type of boat that can be steered without a rudder. Once you're under way with wind directly on your starboard beam and you want to turn left, all you have to do is loosen the mizzen, tighten the jib, loosen the mainsail . . . and the ship falls off to the left! Act in reverse and she'll turn to the right. Since this is all the control you have, though, I don't recommend your trying it except in the open sea.

Ann's ability to cook is truly amazing. I had hung our Mexican dried beef in the forepeak to give it plenty of air through its muslin bag; this "jerky" is tasty enough, and it *is* meat, after all, but its ordinary texture is tough enough to make anyone thankful they still have their teeth! Ann cooked some of it for dinner tonight as the basis for Beef Burgundy with mushrooms, onions, red wine and just the right combination of spices and herbs. She served it over rice, and the meat was as tender and tasty as *filet mignon*. She says her secret is the pressure cooker. Ann's fantastic cooking is proof that you can go to sea without and not miss having refrigeration at all!

Early today I discovered a rip in the mainsail clew. In a confused sea the yard has a tendency to swing up and down. As the ship plows into each wave, the yard sweeps into the air, causing the sail to rip apart in its weakest spot(s). I hove the boat into the wind and lowered the sail. Ann resewed the damaged clew in an hour. All day the wind has been blowing a steady 18 mph, fortunately from the north which lets us make a due west course. I estimate our speed to be about 3 mph.

My longitude sight was way off again. The ones I have, however, indicate progress to the west. I feel confidence in my Polaris sights that put us near 20 degrees north latitude, about the same as Hilo. I intend to follow this latitude by Polaris sights daily straight across. It doesn't make that much difference whether or not I know our longitude. The islands can be seen from fifty miles away and if I'm on the correct latitude I'll find them.

In the sailing days of Columbus, the sailors called that method of navigation "square sailing." One would go north or south until the proper latitude was reached and then turn "squarely" to the right or left, following the chosen latitude on into the port of destination. The Polaris sight is so simple a child can do it. Point the sextant where you imagine the North Star to be. Sight over the compass for the correct direction and move the sextant back and forth across the horizon and suddenly the star will appear in the sextant glass. Then read the degrees and minutes on the scale. That reading of the scale is your latitude! In order to make it a perfect fix, correct for refraction by using a table. For general approximate navigation no correction needs to be applied. The entire operation takes only about ten minutes once you are used to taking the Polaris sighting.

Columbus used this method himself, and once he located one island in the Caribbean he was able to make three more trips there from Spain—always returning to the same "discovered island" once he knew its exact latitude. What was good enough for Columbus was good enough for me.

June 4

We went to bed last night about 10:00 p.m. and slept through the night. I feel we're far enough from the continent to relax. In the light breezes I left the mainsail up with the helm lashed amidships. This morning the boat is creeping along on the same course we set last night, and we progressed a few miles while asleep. Before bedtime, Ann and I played several games of gin; as usual, she won most of them. And I studied contract law during my reading period. I enjoy that because there's no "make believe" in it . . . law isn't fiction. It's reality. Some day, perhaps I'll complete a course of study in law. My father has a complete law library which I plan to use, but I want to wait until after I'm sixty. I don't want to rush back to the treadmill. It's too fulfilling to be off of it.

I didn't wake this morning until broad daylight; I overslept my usual predawn wakeup time. Usually, I get up early, make a cup of coffee and a thermos of tea and then look at the conditions of the sea, the deck, and the sails. I read for a couple of hours and then wake Ann for breakfast. This morning we used a fine butter substitute for the first time: plain lard mixed with two drops of "Wagner's Imitation Butter Flavoring." She mixed our imitation butter with rice—rice is a good basis for anything! —Maggi Sauce (a Swiss concoction), salt, pepper, and sprinkled it with Parmesan cheese. A wonderful breakfast!

I hate fishing but am trying to learn how to fish. No luck yet. Today I kept a lure over the side and watched all kinds of fish inspect it. I didn't see one fish express any interest in it whatsoever. Today there were iridescent fish—blue, yellow-green with turquoise fins and yellow tails—swimming gaily all around the boat. A three-foot wide turtle joined them this morning close to the stern. He poked his head out of the water to look at me straight in the eye and then slowly paddled away. He came back,

24

and I stood poised with my gaff hook attached to the end of a boat hook. My one lunge to snare him missed. He gave me a reproachful look, lowered his head, and swam off. Then an eight-foot long shark—with pilot fish swimming over its back—circled the boat and made a threatening pass towards where I was standing on deck. From three feet aft, it stared at me with its "fish-eye" look and departed. I don't think I want to go swimming or fall overboard. I'm afraid of sharks.

June 5

I know I should learn how to fish. Today, I really tried. I kept a line over the side all day and caught nothing. There are so many fish swimming alongside and underneath that it seems I ought to be able to catch at least *one*, but I can't! The yellowtails won't even look at my trout lure. I also tried a white feather lure today and had no luck. I trail them close enough to the boat so that I can see both the lure and the fish. I even put out the lure Don said would be guaranteed to bring me a fish—the red-and-white "pike." It worked immediately for him several months ago when he illustrated its apparently irresistible attraction to fish. When *I* tried it then during his demonstration efforts, I landed a one-eyed baby shark and nothing else. Today, the yellowtails seemed quite uninterested in this lure. Maybe one would have snatched it, but a ten-foot long shark sneaked near and all the other fish rushed away. He was enormous. I grabbed the line and pulled the lure away from the shark, afraid he might bite it. Maybe it was these huge sharks that had been breaking my line these past few days?

Ann and I stashed away one jug of wine and a bottle of Rice tea (a potent tequila-tasting liquor that we'd gotten for an outrageously cheap price in Yelapa). We'll save the gallon of Mexican vino tinto wine for the first sighting of Hawaii and the liquor for our first night anchored in the Bay near Hilo.

June 6

Before sunrise this morning, I was pleased to see that we're still on course, helm lashed, making a steady 2 mph in light favorable airs. As usual I turned on the kerosene stove for my coffee and tea and then walked around on my inspection tour. A flying fish soared over the boat and hit the deck! I grabbed it immediately and shouted for Ann to come and see. Her sleepy voice came from below to tell me to use it for bait. She was definitely not ready for breakfast. I used its head and tail for bait and within five minutes, I had a strike! I reeled in a modest-sized yellowtail. I got him on deck without losing him and called Ann again to come up and see my silvery prize. If was my first "legitimate" catch of edible fish! No answer this time. I filleted two pieces—one from each side—and cooked it with Ann's herb sauce, lemon butter, some spices, potatoes, and onions. Ann enjoys eating fish even less than I do, but she gamely announced that it was delicious. Maybe it was the breakfast in bed that she enjoyed more, though.

Light northerly winds continue, course southwest by west. I hope we soon hit the trades where the wind blows from the northeast. This will put the wind on our after starboard quarter where the *Felucca* sails her best. My *Frisco Felluca II* is quite a ship! Here she is, sailing with confidence and cheer—almost smugly! She's steering herself in one of the most beautiful days and the most perfect sea I've ever seen. How can people get so lucky?

Ann and I play chess or gin rummy everyday. Some days we play both. Before long I'll have to ask her for a handicap. Either game is good mental exercise and is enjoyable and competitive but friendly pastime. I think cruising couples should play these kinds of games together. I also think that besides tending to the ship's duties, the cruising individual should *create* something each day, something like scrimshaw, learning new knots (mine are from Ashley's *Book of Knots*), drawing, writing, sewing, or reading. If a sailor occupies his or her time this way, s/he's not likely to feel boredom or loneliness. To me, the time between sunup and sundown seems short. Some days it's too short. Of course, it helps to have a store of memories of good times, good sailing, and good people to recall together. Ann and I certainly have an abundant supply of these!

Later

These recent days have been positively idyllic. Before Ann and I began this voyage, I'd been led to believe—by many people who wrote books and articles about their crossing the Pacific in a small boat and by having had many actual conversations with those who've done it—that our crossing would be fraught at least with inconvenience and discomfort, if not with actual problems and dangers. But so far—knock on wood—our crossing has been one in which each day is more pleasurable and enjoyable than the preceding one. And I'm counting the entire time we spent in preparation for this crossing.

We actually started this cruise almost two years ago without really knowing it. When we first left Sausalito, all we intended to do was explore the Sacramento River Delta and see what the *Frisco Felucca II* could do. We sailed out of San Francisco Bay into the river one day with no serious thoughts about going further than the Delta and no plans at all about how long we'd stay away from Sausalito. And now, we were well under way for months in Our Trip. Mexico was behind us and Hawaii was ahead!

I remember how exhilarating it was in those first few days of cruising around the Delta, having my felucca ghosting along under full sail for the first time. She was surprisingly easy to set on any course—against the wind, with the wind, any direction I wanted her to go. She'd head off proudly and cheerfully, eagerly accepting my directives. On the very first day, the wind was from the south at about 25 mph, making whitecaps throughout San Pablo Bay and giving us an excellent slant to sail to Vallejo. At first, I had been a little scared to hoist the huge mainsail, but I'd gritted my teeth and hauled her up. The sail was so much larger than I'd been used to, and I had shuddered to think that it was too big for my new boat, that it would pull us over in the first hard gust of wind. However, as I pulled it, that main lateen sail quickly filled smoothly and tightly with the wind, and its eucalyptus yard curved from the air pressure into a perfect foil. The boat lunged forward, heeling only about 15 degrees (because of the five tons of ballast I'd installed?). I remarked to Ann that, in spite of my excitement to be under way in my new boat, I was quite aware of my fear. To be sure, it wasn't much, but it was very real.

Fear is something any sailor experiences when s/he enters new waters or sails in a brand new boat into even familiar waters, and I've learned that a certain amount of fear is appropriate. There are serious questions with a new boat, such as how much sail can she take before she keels over? Will she come about easily in the wind? How will she take the current? And so on. New waters could be hiding new dangers just below the surface. New currents could carry the boat far out to sea. So many factors are involved with a new boat and with new waters that anyone in his right mind would be scared—at least a *little* bit. But I figured that anybody who can't handle that fear, anybody who denies that fear or who can't deal with it, probably can't meet those unknown possibilities if they happen. Those people probably ought to stay anchored safely at home.

I remember very clearly that first day we left to begin our cruise into the Delta Country. That was the day we had our very first indication that our *Felucca* was something quite special beyond what we already knew. The wind was directly off our starboard beam as Ann hung onto the wheel with calm determination. I could tell she was tasting that fear, too, and that she was using it to help her steer directly and firmly for Carquinas Bridge four miles ahead at Vallejo. She was doing her job well, and she was trusting me to do mine. After about ten minutes, she announced, "I haven't had to touch the wheel since I started! She's steering herself!"

I took the wheel from Ann, thinking perhaps her magic touch that she has with so many other things extended to the wheel of my new boat and that she was simply exaggerating the abilities of my pride and joy. But to my genuine amazement the *Frisco Felucca II was* steering herself! I lashed the wheel, thinking I'd lock us into the course the boat was taking and then add corrections as needed. Lo and behold, not even minor corrections were necessary. Yes, the wind stayed constant both in speed and direction, more or less, but the boat did steer itself merrily all the way to Vallejo. Self-steering devices on other boats often go haywire and take the boat far off course unless they're watched carefully, but *my* self-steering device was the entire boat herself!

I hadn't tried to create an automatic pilot. I thought I'd created a sailboat. All I'd done was convert an old lifeboat to a sailboat, adding what seemed necessary. And I'd not added everything all at once. The required basics came first and then I'd simply added or adapted things as I discovered, through experience, the most effective way to sail this particular vessel on a straight course. I think the secret ingredient in this standard mixture is the not-so-standard lateen rigging, because I had obviously created a *balanced rig* that truly steered itself. What's a balanced rig? Darned if I knew at the time. It's just that I didn't know what else to call it. Most sailors never get their boat to steer itself; those who do usually buy an automatic pilot, an expensive device to install, and they have to follow elaborate instructions to do this and to do that with many parts and pieces of their boats to get it to work even some of the time. But I'd practically discovered gold nuggets! My *Felucca* had her own "automatic pilot," and it was herself! Ann and I celebrated this minor miracle with a special meal, laid on a real table cloth with a bottle of our special wine and a lit candle for romance, and we toasted the *Felucca* again and again throughout our happy meal.

It was a boatload of pride that sailed up the channel to Vallejo: a proud skipper, a proud crew, and a proud boat with red, white and green flying jib in sharp contrast with her off-white canvas lateen sails. Hours later, the *Felucca* was still under her uncanny self-steerage as we approached the bridge near Vallejo, and when I took over the wheel to turn left into the Mare Island Channel I confirmed that the boat had come the entire way with very little drift even though the wind was directly on our beam (that was when the thought occurred to me: no larger keel needed—just leeboards). A short time after I took the wheel, we drew abeam of the famous old Vallejo Yacht Club and I threw out the anchor. The *Felucca* turned sharply on a reverse course as the anchor spun her around and brought her to an abrupt halt. We had arrived.

We changed right away into our dress blues and disembarked into a sparkling world of good times and relaxation at the Club and its related environs. As we arrived, I couldn't help but notice a large crowd of club members and guests at the Yacht Club who were lined along the railing, pointing with wide-eyed interest at us. Some of these people told me later that they were fascinated by our unusual boat, calling it "an apparition from the past." Ann and I were very proud of the *Felucca*, and we both knew very well that it was just a $150 used, galvanized old iron lifeboat from some ship, an old boat that Ann and I had worked very hard to make into a seaworthy and comfortable sailing vessel. I'd put tons of cement ballast in her hold, and she was quite solid; the

Felucca was a fine sailing vessel. Having been with the *Felucca* since her birth, so to speak, we were quite used to her "uniqueness." This visit at the Yacht Club started a long series of interested favorable and positive comments about what we were sailing. It was pleasant.

Happily, there was no schedule we planned to follow, no deadlines to meet, and no particular place we had to be, so we stayed at the Yacht Club for some time, enjoying the members, other guests, and some truly fine entertainment.

At one point, not too long after our arrival, a military official from Mare Island came over to the *Felucca* and demanded to know why our boat was anchored here. "Get it out," he commanded. "This is a restricted area. You can't stay here." He told us that atomic submarines were manufactured on the island and that no one was allowed to anchor nearby. We protested that we were guests at the Yacht Club, but he insisted we moved into the designated Yacht Club mooring area. Perhaps the *Felucca* charmed even the military, because we moved only a few hundred feet and nobody came back to tell us to move again. Perhaps it was the boat or perhaps it was the middle-aged couple on it, the couple who spent their time on the boat in junk clothes and who would row ashore dressed to the nines—blue blazer with slacks and tie on the man and handmade designer clothes on the beautiful woman—or perhaps it was just the way things worked out at the time. We laughed about making a vivid point to clean up when we went out; we didn't believe in going out in junk clothes! At any rate, we stayed several days anchored near the Yacht Club and the nuclear submarine factory, thoroughly enjoying the good times provided by the water, the weather, and the wonderfully generous and gregarious members of the Vallejo Yacht Club. Then, one cheerful sunny morning with a brisk breeze, we pulled anchor and headed out.

The days turned into weeks as we explored the area around Sacramento known as the "Delta Country" along the Sacramento River. We visited every place we could, including Sacramento, Stockton, Pittsburg, Benicia, Napa, Petaluma, and other towns and cities, as well as practically every other byway and bayou we could find. There are at least 800 miles of beautiful waterways in the Delta. One can cruise places so remote in the Delta that they are hardly changed since Indians used them as hunting and

30

fishing sites, or places quite populous as well. If one wants, one can find profound solitude or a profusion of friendly natives and other sailors in these ubiquitous waters. The Delta is a place not to be missed, a place I recommend to others as one of California's "must-see" areas.

We put up the sails at every opportunity as we slowly wound our way through the Delta Country. If the wind died or if the current and or tides were adverse for sailing, we moved slowly by using one or both of our two five-horsepower outboards installed in the inboard wells. Of course, our speed varied while we were under sail, and we cruised along with the engine at about three to three and one-half mph, and we used engine power only when we thought it was absolutely necessary. I still think today what I thought then: a sailboat has no use for an engine. I had added the engines as an afterthought, thinking that mechanical power might come in handy in an emergency. Even so, I hadn't been able to afford a full size inboard engine, so I went the least expensive route and installed the first outboard that I could buy and that would fit with another into the inboard well. I secured it to stay straightaway and steered the boat up on deck with the wheel. Yes, the engine smoke and fumes would bother us if we were below, but we were usually above—and we used the engine so seldom—that we never had a major problem in this area. The mere *sound* of any engine on any boat grates on my ears at any time, but it practically hurts my teeth when I hear it coming from a sailing vessel. I closed my ears and held my teeth when I used my own engine; I justify it by thinking there's no other choice if I want to move from a dead calm or escape an otherwise unescapable sailing problem. When we finally got back to Sausalito, I sold the engines. I just don't like engines on sailboats.

Our first anchorage after the Vallejo Yacht Club—for any length of time, anyway—was in Frank's Tract Lake next to Bethel Island. It was one of Nature's paradise gardens. The glorious Indian summer weather prevailed that year until the end of December, giving us bright, sparkling clear and sunny weather day after day. We marvelled continuously at the enduring peace all around us. We reveled in such things as the regular morning and evening flying platoons of wild birds overhead and around us on the water as they tended their private purposes with such diligence and grace. At times, the sky was significantly darkened with peppery flocks of wild geese, ducks, seagulls, mudhens, pheasants, and other types of birds we couldn't name as they rushed to and fro. People told us, too, that the entire area was teeming with catfish, bass, and sturgeon that could grow to unusually great lengths, luring fishermen from all over the country to enjoy Nature's bounty.

I had rigged our 14-foot black skiff with two rowing stations—four oars—so that two of us could row at the same time, and Ann and I could move it swiftly and with sharp control, seldom needing to discuss which way to go or how hard to row. It was a beautiful little boat, made even more beautiful because of how we used it and where it took us. We used it to spend hours every day exploring every nook and cranny of Frank's Tract Lake and Bethel Island. Word spread quickly that we were from Sausalito, and that worked in our favor. Folks around there had the idea that Sausalito people were somehow different, that they were quite artistic with "bohemian attitudes," and they routinely welcomed us with open and eagerly curious arms. They quickly let us know they were fascinated with what I had come to call "my character boat," and they seemed to enjoy this curious couple who so quickly had come to admire them and their special lake. The charms of Frank's Tract Lake worked well on us, so we decided to stay there for the winter. I hadn't yet become accustomed to living year-round on my small boat, so we sort of automatically decided, without serious consideration for anything else, to find a house to stay in. We soon found a small house on stilts at Dutch Slough that included an adequate dock for the *Felucca* and her skiff, and by the end of December, we were warming by the fireplace in our own house on land. Every day that offered any sailing whatsoever was a day we'd leave the comforts of that cottage and explore the waters and adjacent land areas, and we met large numbers of wonderful people everywhere we went.

The San Joaquin Yacht Club was one of our major hangouts. I played my cornet there many times, danced with Ann—and many other charming, delightful, and beautiful women—feasted on baked iced sturgeon and other fantastically delicious delicacies, and made friends with those we stayed in touch with afterwards. We'd run into other "anchor outs" at the local pubs, too; one of these, Jerry Biesel, refused to sail and preferred a high-powered motorboat instead. Jerry, a doctor, was one of the many high-lights of those months, and he became so dependent on the hair-cuts Ann gave him that he tracked her down wherever we might be, either driving or coming around any distance in one of his boats to get his haircut. For some time, he followed us around the Delta, showing up somewhere to meet Ann for the haircut. He was one of the friends who was chagrined that we planned to take Our Trip and leave the country. We received a letter many months later from a mutual friend that Jerry had died unexpect-edly. He was a good man and we miss him yet today.

As we continued to enjoy the company of so many warmhearted and friendly people, plans for Our Trip began to take specific shapes. We discussed the plans with our new friends and began to see some reasonable semblance of plans for a trip we could actually make. Our Trip eventually became our trip of a lifetime, and it began as thoughts expressed with friends on and around Frank's Tract Lake. Our Trip quickly became a plan that would get us to Mexico, wending our way slowly down the Pacific Coast, and ending at, say, Puerto Vallarta. Of course, so long as we were in a house away from the ocean, Our Trip was only talk, but we talked about it every chance we got. We got advice, opinions, and all kinds of suggestions.

Even the "Motorcycle Man," who had been on a boat perhaps three times in his life, had his suggestions. "Gordon," as we called him, was notorious for his mindless driving. He'd had the unfortu-nate experience of having committed vehicular homicide (and having had to spend several years in prison for that tragedy), yet he seemed not to have learned any lessons that would improve his driving. No one I knew, including us, accepted his invitation to ride with him on his motorcycle. In general, the main piece of advice we got from him was *not* to take the *Felucca* on Our Trip.

"It'll sink in the first storm," he said. "You'll never get to land unless you learn more about specific navigation techniques," he said. "That lateen rig can't take the winds out in the Pacific," he said. Gordon and other friends said things like that, on and on, over and over. Ann and I seemed to be the only people who took seriously the plans for Our Trip to Mexico. Actually, our friends *must* have thought we could actually make Our Trip successfully, because nobody makes suggestions to people when there's no real chance for success (remember the old saying, "Nobody makes suggestions to losers?"), but if they did, they didn't tell us. At least, we'd managed to crystallize our plans to the point where we firmly decided to sail south to Mexico.

There was a handful of Yacht Club members in particular who looked on Our Trip with unabashed cynicism and amusement. They were convinced my "character boat" would never make it to Mexico on the open sea, and they took perverse pleasure in watching us surge past the Club during a strong wind or even a violent storm, lateen sail taut in winds so strong that they made the boat pitch violently as if it were a bucking bronco trying to toss off its riders. But even they offered some suggestions. Even they could see that this couple who were so obviously enjoying all they could enjoy were determined enough so that perhaps they just might possibly defeat the odds and truly make it to Mexico in that funny boat.

We gave these naysayers frequent causes to wonder about our sanity, including taking the *Felucca* out in every strong wind from a bluster to a storm. Storms were a treat for us. We looked forward to them so that we could learn as much as we could about the boat before we left for Our Trip. I figured that a storm in the Delta provided excellent opportunities to teach necessary lessons to us two students in a classroom that was far better protected than the open Pacific. The worst that could happen in a Delta storm would be that we might be blown into the weeds or badly off course. Nothing could be truly life-threatening. There was always *somebody* close by in case we ever needed help. So each time a storm from a gale to a thunderstorm to a cloudy day with lots of wind and rain seemed imminent, Ann and I would stock the boat, put on our foul weather gear, take off from our sheltered dock and leave the Slough to whatever unknown adventures the winds would take us. More than once as we visited with friends at the Yacht Club, the sky would begin to darken and the wind would begin to gust and a friend would say something like, "Well, T. Jay, a storm's coming. I guess you crazy folks are gonna go sailing." I'd answer, "Yep, looks like some good sailing," and off we'd go to see how heavy a wind the *Felucca* could take and still float. I was determined to make Our Trip a reality, and we had decided to use this winter as the only shakedown cruise we'd take before that reality came about.

Our lease expired on the house that following spring, and when it did we moved aboard the *Felucca*. We've been living here ever since. Living aboard let us continue our exploration of the Delta's waterways without interruption, going farther with our travels and learning more about the boat, meeting new and interesting people along the way. All that, and we never left home. Living aboard also meant that we didn't have to wait for either storms or the wind; they came to us. And sometimes they came to us without giving us the warning we'd come to rely on when we lived in the cottage.

One sunny evening when the breeze died, we anchored in a small inlet not far from Frank's Tract Lake and settled in for a calm, comfortable night. We had the garlic minced and the fire going for the beef when a major blast of wind suddenly blew across us from the north, immediately forcing us to secure everything and postpone dinner. We'd laid both 25-pound Danforth and 80-pound Yachtsman anchors off the bow on the windward side of a tiny bay, alongside a berm (a narrow ledge of soft, grassy tufts of mud and dirt). Quickly after the strong wind started, I checked both anchors and assured myself that they would hold all night, thinking that even a 60 mph wind wouldn't be enough to dislodge us. Because of the wind's tossing and heaving the boat, it took more time than we'd planned to complete our dinner (although we enjoyed it leisurely enough) and turn in for the night, secure and warm inside under blankets with the chill of a howling wind outside.

I woke with a start from a sound sleep in the middle of the night by a violent, jerking motion of the boat and a series of sickening thumps. I jumped out of bed, opened the hatch, and saw the incredible: we were dragging straight downwind across the inlet to the opposite berm. Both anchors were dragging together, cooperating with the wind. There was nothing to do but hold on and watch the *Felucca* ride stern first up onto the berm. We imbedded in the mud with a loud slurping noise as the boat gave an almost audible sigh.

"At least we're not dragging anymore," I said to Ann, and since we seemed secure enough now, we went back to sleep. The next morning, I literally fell out of the bunk. When I peeked out the hatch, I saw that the tide was the lowest I'd seen in some time, and we were sitting at a cock-eyed angle in the mud. Wild grasses surrounded the boat. After we got dressed, we found that the mud was too deep for us even to walk away from the boat. We were stuck. High and dry.

About 10:00 that morning, after the tide had come in, we were startled—and quite pleased, considering the circumstances—to hear the sound of a motor. It came close, and we saw that it was on a sturdy 6-foot wide working rowboat which was handled by a cowboy. He was sharp-looking in his gloves, Levis, and cowboy boots, with a Stetson-looking hat that shielded his piercing light blue eyes and completed the cowboy image.

"Need some help?" he shouted.

"Sure do," I shouted back. "Can you get aboard for a cup of coffee?"

The tide had come in enough for him to get his boat next to ours, and he came on. His name was Duke, and he was the ramrod of a thousand-acre island in the Delta where he grew corn, squash, and other row crops. He's an ex-bronco buster and has led a very interesting life, colorful enough (I think) to be the subject of at least one movie. After coffee, heavy cream, and croissants, the Duke left to cross the Slough and get one of his workmen with a second outboard boat. The two men returned and tied the *Felucca* to both their boats and pulled her off the berm like two cowboys dragging a reluctant steer through a corral gate. When we were clear, the Duke explained why anchors will not hold properly in peat ground bottoms; the safest way to anchor securely in such a bottom is to run a line ashore to a willow branch, then set at least one anchor offshore, leaving the boat to stand between the two. This is what we did, and we stayed for several days.

The Duke was an excellent host. He thoroughly enjoyed his island and his work with his crops, and he filled us with good food, good stories, and good times. When we left, he gave us several boxes of freshly picked asparagus, squash, tomatoes, wonderfully sweet sweet corn, and a special present of a newly plucked wild goose.

Eventually, we left Duke's island, meandering down the Slough to yet another landfall, learning more and more about the marvelous *Felucca* almost everyday and meeting yet more and more wonderful people at each turn. At the next island, we met a yachtsman, Walt Vorhees, whom we had met earlier before we'd left Sausalito. He lived here with his red-haired lady friend, and

36

we accepted his invitation to tie up at his dock next to their quaint old cottage that overlooked both the 800-acre island and the waterway. As we were tying off, Walt shouted, "We're going to a party tonight in Mill Valley. How about coming with us?"

Ann and I were delighted at the prospect and accepted his invitation immediately; we were onshore in our party clothes, ready to go in record time. Right away, we drove with Walt and his friend to San Francisco so that he could get something from his apartment in North Beach and so that he could switch from the car he was driving to another of his cars. I was overwhelmed with the car he selected to use. It was his "town car," a bright red 1937 German Horsch phaeton. Needless to say, the Horsch was in excellent condition. It was larger than the largest Mercedes Benz I'd ever seen and had two huge spoked-wheel spare tires, one mounted just to the rear of both front fenders. The trunk was leather with a chrome carrying rack on the outside. We drove in elegant style with the top down, crossing the Golden Gate Bridge into Marin County with what I felt sure were the envying eyes of every other motorist gazing at us. I thought we must have been the cynosure of the evening in that classic automobile, and I kept thinking what a treat Walt was giving these two saltwater sailors.

We stayed a while near Walt's island until the beginning of February. Then we spent the rest of the spring and early summer cruising elsewhere around the Delta, enjoying to the fullest the people, the waters, and the countryside. We continued to learn what the *Felucca* would and would not do in this kind of weather and that kind, and we learned why cruising the Delta in the spring is so often considered idyllic. It was truly wonderful. Most of the country we saw was either marshland or woodlands, and what wasn't was rich farmland with roads along levees next to the water. Charming old farmhouses dotted the landscape. Frequently, we'd see farmers and fishermen in pickup trucks and small boats as they stopped to gawk at my "character boat." As we inched down the Petaluma and Suisun Rivers, I felt as if we were in a tight narrow canal; there were no levees and the land came almost right up to both sides of the boat in several places. The pastoral countryside didn't seem to notice the *Felucca* sailing serenely past, but we certainly noticed the countryside.

The scenery that includes both forks of the Mokelumne River

was among the loveliest. The spring weather was soft and gentle in the Delta that year, and the greenery as well as the flowers were the most lavish the Delta had seen in years. On the north fork of the Mokelumne, beyond two drawbridges, is a blue-green everglade known locally as "the meadows." Hundreds of leafy trees overhang the water from both shores and some passages are almost like man-made tunnels through the verdant woods, opening up onto broad, grassy meadows next to the placid waters. In summer or autumn heat, these meadows provide a fine resting place for those who tie up nearby (as Ann and I did for many days). It's a marine paradise of sorts, and scores of sailboats, houseboats, and motorboats anchor throughout the area and enjoy the peace of "the meadows."

That spring, Ann and I discovered why other people had cautioned us about the vagaries of unexpected tides, currents, and hazards in this beautiful place. When high water rushes down from the High Sierra and the Delta's waters rise to flood level, the combination of tides and current create conditions that can ruin the voyages of even the most experienced sailors. We had exceptionally high water and unpredictable currents to contend with at times, but we were both *determined* not to let anything ruin Our Trip. Nothing did. When we were faced with something we'd not dealt with before, we'd run with it, still trying to learn more about what the *Felucca* would do in all kinds of weather. After all, we certainly didn't want to undertake Our Trip without as much knowledge about and experience with such things as we could possibly get.

When things got difficult we'd simply wait. If we were sailing, we'd drop the anchor and wait. If we were ashore, we'd produce something pleasant to do and wait. What were we waiting for? We were sailors, and we were waiting for just one thing: more favorable sailing conditions. This slow pace, even when enforced at random upon us by the weather, was one of the most rewarding parts of Delta cruising for us.

On one occasion, we waited two full days for favorable tide, currents, and wind simply to cross the river. We had anchored across from Vince Continente's Driftwood (a waterfront bar and grill at Pittsburg), and the river was aboil with flotsam and jetsam that swirled dangerously in eddies and contradicting currents caused by the unusually large Sierra runoff and heavy local rains. Both the Sacramento and San Joaquin Rivers (which meet at Pittsburg) were well above ordinary levels, and we waited for the most favorable steady northwest wind. When I was reasonably sure we had it, we plunged across the muddy, roiling river with storm sail up and mainmast and red spritsail under the bowsprit. Columbus had used this combination on his caravel the *Nina*, and I kept thinking, "If he could do it, so can I." The steady 35 mph wind pushed us swiftly past Pittsburg against 6 mph current, and we managed to avoid each dangerous eddy and uncontrolled floating log and other debris that filled the churning water. As we sailed under Antioch Bridge, running with the wind and dodging the debris, the drawbridge master gave us a "well done" toot on the bridge horn.

We spent several months lazing around the Delta and in midsummer, as we headed east on the San Joaquin River fifteen miles out of Stockton, we spied a familiar tugboat across from us, heading in the opposite direction. It was the *Loafer* from Sausalito, and "Dredge (the owner)" and "Captain Garbage" (the *Loafer's* crew and "Dredge's" good friend) recognized us about the same time we recognized them. They pulled around, caught our line, and came aboard for a while. It must have been quite a sight from land: my unusual looking *Felucca*, moving majestically but with a battered old tugboat twice our size under tow behind us.

The channel we were in comes to its end at a highway bridge in front of Stockton's municipal buildings. We looked forward to staying a few days in and around Stockton and we stayed three months. At the end of the channel was a sign, "Uptown Yacht Harbor," and on the dock beneath stood several people. One of these people was smiling and waving energetically to us, calling, "Bring her right in here, Captain. You can tie up if you wish. We've been watching you sail up the river. Your boat looks great!"

The man who shouted was wearing a red and white–striped tee-shirt, suntan cords and a dashing black captain's hat. He had sparkling brown eyes and a most unusual growth of hair on his upper lip. Most men who wear a moustache don't look all that much different from other men who wear one, but this man's moustache was unique; It was waxed to a silky polish, and each end curled into a small, neat black circle. He looked very much like a pirate on a Mediterranean felucca from at least the fifteenth century.

"Thanks very much, sir, but we will anchor down a hundred yards. We'll come ashore and see you this evening," I shouted back to him.

By the time we dropped anchor, the customers in a motel adjoining the channel—as well as yachtsmen in the harbor, passengers from the bus station on the opposite shore, and numerous others—were lined up on the bridge and jetties to observe our craft. Some were cheering, some shouted, some applauded, but none jeered.

Later that evening, we officially met the man who had first shouted to us. His name was Sal Cerbone, ebullient owner of the Uptown Yacht Harbor, a self-described "Bahstin boy," and he invited us into his living quarters to visit. They were in back of his harbor office, and they had broad picture windows that overlooked his boat docks and the San Joaquin waterway. He had heard me playing my cornet earlier and had asked me to play for him this time, and I did forthwith.

He was a drummer, he said. There were a high-hat cymbal set and snare drum set up in one corner of his roomy quarters, and against one wall was a small upright piano, hammers showing, top garlanded with multi-colored cloth ball fringe. Above his bed hung an enormous black and white photograph, larger than life, of a French actress in a thin, very wet and revealing dress. A caged Nynah bird regularly yelled, "Baby Doll, Baby Doll," and then whistled that familiar shrill riff that men sometimes use to attract the attention of a beautiful woman. Sal was a wonderful cook, and he and Ann gathered together more than once in his kitchen to cook a new dish. One of the new recipes they invented, "Chicken Salaam," is fried floured chicken which is baked for two hours in a garlic and mushroom sauce and flavored with vermouth and Italian herbs. Delicious! Sal and Ann's cooking had become legendary among people who knew them.

Sal showed Ann how to use the high hat and snare drum. She is a natural at keeping an even "two-beat" rhythm (accent on the second and fourth beats). He rigged a "gut bucket," made of a big old-fashioned galvanized tub placed upside down with a three-foot piece of gut string attached to the center and then in turn attached to the far end of the bottom handle that was embedded in the bottom of the tub. This gut-bucket, played like a bass fiddle, made an excellent addition to our three-piece combo. We went through several old standards, including "Five Foot Two," "Twelfth Street Rag," and "It's A Sin To Tell A Lie." Sal played the gut bucket and sang and danced with expertise, furious mugging, and Jerry Colonna imitations.

Sal was a wonderful host, an amusing guy. Yachting people flocked to his Uptown Yacht Harbor to talk and laugh with him. On weekends fifteen or more luxurious yachts would be put into the harbor. Occasionally, musicians were aboard, and one balmy afternoon a trombone player showed up—these are very difficult to find! Sal trotted over to me saying, "T. Jay, you and Ann come over and join us. I've found a trombone player!"

I grabbed my cornet and headed for the bar. The high hat and drum were laid out for Ann. Sal had a cymbal and bell "stick" that rang merrily with each stamp of the stick on the floor. He rhythmically beat it up and down while dancing and gyrating like an animated elf, entertaining everyone. Not only was there a trombone player this day, but there was also an excellent clarinetist. He was Russ Cline, a professional musician who owned a Sacramento music store and led a youth marching band. He had played clarinet with Jack Teagarden in the 1940s. With this elite combination of musicians, we romped through such tunes as "When You're Smiling," "Black and Blue," "Baby Face," "St. Louis Woman," and many more. Both old-timers and young kids loved our music. Many guests danced on the dock. Some visited aboard the *Felucca*. Though most of these new friends didn't quite believe we planned to take "that boat thing" out into the ocean, they were polite and wished us well.

Several days passed when Sal offered me the use of his tools and workshop to complete my building the *Felucca II* and outfitting her for the open sea. By this time, we had been telling everyone we met, including Sal, about Our Trip and about how we had plans to leave for the open southern waters no later than late this year. I happily accepted his kind offer, working with his shop tools on the boat for two months, buttressing the eight portholes for hard weather, finishing various details below deck, and generally getting her as tight as possible. I was trying to make that boat as seaworthy as she could possibly be. That ship was going to cross the Pacific one of these days. I think I knew it then, even though I might not have mentioned it to anyone.

The Delta trip turned into a year and then some. We learned

41

a lot about the *Felucca* and in the process found that we wanted to keep sailing her. And we've kept sailing her. From Sausalito through the Delta, stop off in Sausalito to change clothes, then out the Golden Gate to Mexico. Now here we are heading across the Pacific to Hawaii. This voyage just keeps getting better and better.

June 7

Aboard every ship there's always something to replace or repair. My predawn inspection showed our mainsail clew in the aft corner in poor condition again. We worked on it from about 6:00 a.m. until noon. Ann sewed a light rope in a fold inside the leach to beef up the mainsail and clew. She was exhausted by the time she finished. And in spite of my strong dislike of going into the water where sharks are, I went over the side and put shackles on the rudder chain.

I took a Polaris sight last night and another at noon today, one degree (sixty miles) apart. We are beating upwind in light northwest airs. I don't want to lose any more latitude than necessary to reach the trades. Spent the night in a flat calm with yards slatting noisily.

Today the sea is a heavenly blue, temperature in the middle seventies. Yellowtails swim back and forth under the boat. I keep changing lures but no luck. No wonder I don't like fishing. Good thing neither Ann nor I really likes to eat fish.

June 8

This morning the wind shifted to come from the north, enabling the *Felucca* to steer herself west. I checked her course, adjusted the wheel to the new set of her sails, lashed the helm, and left her alone. As long as the wind comes from the same direction, this ship stays on her course indefinitely! Fifteen years ago, at home in Sausalito, I owned one of the famous racing "R" boats. I couldn't get her to steer herself on any point of the wind. At one period of time, I also had a 40-foot baldheaded schooner (no topsails). She couldn't steer herself either. However, each of the three lateen-rigged boats I've had so far, including my beautiful *Frisco Felucca II*, could steer themselves on many points of the compass with the wheel lashed. Lateen sailing is a "curiosity" that allows Ann and me to lounge in comfort together in the saloon below instead of hanging on the wheel, steering a fighting boat. And self-steering has totally eliminated the need for a crew member to stand watches.

Later

No need to stand watches? Well, I have to qualify this statement! I realize what a gloriously beautiful day it is out here on the Pacific this June 8 and how short our memories sometimes can be if we're not careful. Not too many months earlier, we got a stern lesson about the need to stand watch. We'd just sailed out of Ensenada, Mexico, with a paying passenger (our strongbox was almost empty, and he paid cash), and while he was with us my nonchalance about standing watches was rebuked firmly.

Our passenger was not a fellow sailor but an American on business in Ensenada. The magic of that sleepy port had gotten to him, and he wanted to experience the pleasures of sailing for the few days he had free. The charm and romance of sailing had captured him. We met many land-bound people in many ports who had been lured by that siren and wanted to come with us. This passenger was one of the few we took aboard for any length of time. He spent almost two weeks with us before his business schedule caught up with him and he had to disembark, and he especially enjoyed short periods of standing watch.

About the time we cleared the shore, all wind stopped. It just stopped, and we were left dead in the water. After seventy-two hours we could still see the town of Ensenada, and I realized with sudden revelation that I had learned *patience*! This "delay" was no bother! No engine and no wind had slowed us down, but so what? I now believe that developing patience and a calm attitude are fundamental keys to survival at sea under any and all conditions. And for us, the fun of sailing had come at its fullest when we found ourselves doing exactly what sailors had done for the centuries before engines existed. Now all that was true for us and still is, and as profoundly comforting as it was to know, we began

43

to get bored. As Ann pointed out, seventy-two hours in one lifetime isn't much—unless, perhaps, it's spent doing the same things over and over without respite no matter how pleasurable those things may be in shorter doses.

Other boats passed by frequently with their motors purring or roaring. None offered us a tow, and I asked for none. On the fourth day of trying to sail out of the bay, the weather turned foggy and the wind shifted enough to allow us to get going on a tack. The tack was planned to take us past Todos Santos Island into the ocean so that we could turn left and have the wind behind us. I felt no particular apprehension in the daytime fog and none when night fell. After all, I was used to sailing in San Francisco Bay and was no stranger to the perils of fog on the water, day or night. And I'd become quite familiar with Mexico's Todos Santos Island, the Bay, and Punta Banda Rock. I had a good compass bearing and was convinced that we were sailing out into the Pacific, headed away from land. All this helped lull me into a general sense of confidence that all was well. Again the *Felucca* sailed herself with her helm lashed while Ann, our passenger, and I puttered around the boat.

Ann prepared a marvelous dinner and we enjoyed our passenger's company while we dined. He pretty much took it upon himself to cast a searching eye around the boat every so often, reporting to me what he saw. His report invariably indicated that he saw nothing except the beauty that was in the sea all around us. However, this night, about 10 p.m., when our passenger went up on deck to look around, he shouted back to us, "I see a light! And land! We're right on top of it!"

I scrambled up the ladder and saw at once why he was so excited. We were headed straight into a wall of rock with a light on top! Another hundred yards and we would be smashing into it! Ann and the passenger madly brought down the sails as I rushed to the foredeck and threw over the 40-pound Navy anchor, tangling the line as it sank to the bottom. The three of us must have made a Keystone Cop image as we scrambled madly to clear the line, but the anchor hit bottom. And it held! We were less than ninety yards from that gigantic rock, in the lee of Todos Santos Island, and we spent the remainder of that foggy night listening to the crashing surf on that perpendicular wall of rock.

Our Trip almost ended with a moment's stupidity. I learned

that moment that one can never take that kind of chance at sea. More specifically in that instance, a constant lookout must be maintained—twenty-four hours a day if necessary—in fog or low visibility. My navigational error had brought us into range of the rock (I hadn't considered the effect of the Humboldt current, moving south along the coast at a mile and a half per hour), and those errors can happen any time. But they can be corrected only if there's someone on the boat who's *watching where the boat is going!*

No need to stand watches? If you want to keep your boat, you stand watches.

June 9

The sensation of being hundreds of miles out on the soft blue Pacific is almost indescribable. Years ago, I dreamily imagined successfully sailing a beautiful yacht to Hawaii, buffeted constantly by towering white combers and howling winds in the bright days and dark, starry nights. I imagined how frightened I'd be all the time as I had that exciting adventure. Now here I am actually doing it!

I'm living my dream! And I haven't left home! The *Felucca* is my home. And it's the most wonderful home I've ever lived in, perhaps the first real one. The sea is my backyard and my front, and my neighbors are always next door even when they're thousands of miles away. Everything in the *Felucca* is familiar and intimate. Ann's here, and we have all that we need.

We're far out at sea and everyday feels right. How *wonderful* to be alive and to enjoy such a day! Ann and I are quite used to the pitching and rolling because of our previous voyages—and especially because we were at anchor on that exposed Puerto Vallarta shore for several months! The boat doesn't lurch violently, nothing falls off the shelves, the eight-dollar Mexican kerosene stove sits unsecured on a shelf on the leeward side of the galley—the ship's movement feels solid every moment when she's sailing. Only occasionally will she give a more lusty roll than usual, bringing the sea and horizon bobbing into view through her portholes.

Ann uses the *Felucca* as her office-at-home several hours a day;

she's been banging away at her typewriter now for at least the last four hours. Just another day at home. Or at the office. It's funny, though, as beautiful as this day has been, as sound as we know this boat to be, I have this constant tickling sensation of doubt—fear?—reminding me that if anything goes wrong out here, we have to fix it and fix it well or else we're lost. Now there's a sobering thought! I'll remedy that with a soothing glass of wine and play "Sweet Georgia Brown" to Ann with the sunset as our backdrop.

If she ever stops typing, we can play some gin rummy. I love that game.

Later

Those first days out on the open seas were beautiful. I had plenty of time to tend to what needed tending to aboard, to watch the endless variety of life and movement around me, and to enjoy Ann's company. Before we'd left on this trip, so many people had told us not to go. They were convinced our little boat was too small for the giant Pacific, they were afraid we'd get hopelessly lost, they were sure we'd disappear forever in the endless stretches of the deep ocean. When we were ending our Delta cruise, those naysayers were growing in number. For days, I harbored the secret thought that perhaps they were right, that perhaps such plans to sail the *Felucca* from Sausalito to Mexico were foolish plans indeed.

We visited several old friends along the way and met some new ones as well. One afternoon, nearing Suisun Bay, a motor yacht passed. Surprisingly, the sweet notes of a well-played trombone (shades of Trummy Young, the trombone player for Louis Armstrong's band!) wafted across the water from this impressive vessel. I glanced at her stern and saw the trombone player who had joined us in the jam session in Stockton at Sal's. He gave me a musician's "hello" with a chorus of "Up The Lazy River," and I took up my cornet to play a duet with variations while we sailed side by side down the river.

Further along the way we stopped again at the Vallejo Yacht Club. I'm not at all convinced that the members believed us when we announced that would start Our Trip for Mexico within a month. But they were sailors and gentlemen; not one rude remark this time about our abilities and not one slur against the appearance of the homemade character boat, my *Felucca!*

As we headed south across San Pablo Bay, an expensive sailing yacht from the swanky St. Francis Yacht Club came close and greeted us, engine running above half power to assist him in beating into the wind. I shouted, "Could you please tow us to the next point where I can get a favorable slant for San Francisco?" He promptly threw us a line and proceeded with the tow. As the sun began to set, we were about halfway to the point and the skipper shouted, "I'll have to let you go. My engine is heating up. I'm going to Mexico in two months and I don't want to take a chance of wrecking my engine!" And he let go of our line.

I pondered his comment and the motivation that made him make it. Most yachtsmen with a boat thirty feet long or longer will not move away from the dock without an engine in top working order. Almost no sailing yachtsman heads for Mexico, let alone across the Pacific, unless his engine is in top condition and he has at least a 500-mile fuel capacity aboard. Like Justin, they recognize fear; when fear comes from a genuinely fearful source, it's foolish not to be confident that it can be dissipated with healthy doses of skill, know-how, or downright mechanically helpful things like an engine on a sailboat! Many times when a serious problem hits a sailboat under sail, a skipper can start the engine and simply move away from the problem while under horsepower.

But as I pondered I also discovered something wrong with his philosophy that puts an engine as a major component in a sailboat: when you're really in trouble, the engine may not start and then where are you? If you've relied on the engine to save you throughout your sailing career, you won't be able to get out of trouble when the engine fails to help. You won't know what to do. Every year we get reports like, "Lost at sea with all hands." A sailor ought to be able to take his ship out and bring it back safely without resorting to an engine at any time. If he can do this, he can safely cross any waters anywhere with or without an engine. Others are asking for trouble because no engine is infallible. After all, when one is under sail in a high wind, one must be able to sail or die, with or without an engine. If the engine doesn't work at that critical moment, one needs to know how to survive with just the sails. So I put my faith in the sails, the boat, and the elements—not in an engine. I still dislike having an engine more than I like having one.

At any rate, almost as soon as we were cast off from the tow the wind rose to at least 30 mph and the bay was covered with whitecaps and choppy waves. A storm was on its way. Black clouds covered the entire sky and we could see the lights of Vallejo receding behind us. The lights of Hamilton Field loomed ahead of us to the west. I hoisted the mainsail and the boat fell off a dismaying 30 degrees to the right.

There wasn't a chance of reaching the point this way. I had to keep the sail up to avoid going broadside to the sea and decided to head for shallow water to try to anchor down and ride out the storm. Suddenly the boat heeled at least 15 degrees and I heard the boiling wake make a swishing sound like a river at full spring flood.

Ann shouted, "The wheel came off!"

I climbed up the hatch and saw that my homemade soapbox derby-type steering apparatus was wobbling freely from side to side. In effect, we didn't have a rudder! I jumped to the stern with a line that I secured to a cross stanchion on the idle rudder and tied it off, immobilizing it at a quarter helm. Ann and I stood in the steering well with mouth agape as we observed another incredible trait of the *Felucca*: she righted her course and headed to the west without varying more than two or three degrees! Either the hand of the supernatural was steering the boat in this storm or else the *Felucca* was steering herself *again!* It was obvious the latter was true. We stayed above in the heavy weather for a while to make sure she was steering herself across San Pablo Bay, then we went below and got out the Chablis to toast our masterful ship and her upcoming voyage of Our Trip.

A new confidence grew in us as she bounded across the Bay, unerringly steering herself where Ann had first pointed her course. An hour later we were anchored for the night in shallow water with the mizzen sail left up to head her into the wind. We were quite comfortable with our vessel headed directly into the wind at anchor.

She didn't "roll"; she steadied out slowly and pitched directly into the oncoming waves. With the after lateen sail on the back mast (see the picture), she rode easy. The next morning, after I

48

had repaired the rudder cable and we had consumed Ann's delightful breakfast of eggs Benedict, we were sailing off to Sausalito.

After we entered Richardson Bay off Sausalito, it actually took a few days for us to reach our usual mooring area near Strawberry Point. We took our time and visited friends and old acquaintances who lived in houseboats and sailing boats throughout the Bay. We took some time to get to our anchorage near Gate Six and thus formally complete the voyage we'd begun about a year ago in preparation for Our Trip.

One friend in particular, Ale Eckstrom, was delighted to see us. He was wonderfully appreciative of our stories of the year's cruise in the Delta—as well as singularly supportive of plans for Our Trip. He is one of the last truly eccentric characters left in the Bay. He got his name because he is always seen carrying his beer mug for ale attached to his belt by a lanyard. Dressed in his 17th century leather pants, vest, and cap, he is all bushy red hair, trimmed beard, and bright green eyes—a striking figure. Aboard his 63-foot World War II Crash boat (formerly a high speed rescue vessel), Ale has been anchored out in Richardson's Bay for almost twenty years and commutes back and forth to shore with his lady friend in his New England-type 18-foot dory with inboard motor well.

Ale has remained the same for the past fifteen to twenty years. Knickers, kneesocks and loafers, a colorful vest, and his Bos'n's whistle attached to the lapel of his vest continue to set off his greying red hair and full but trimmed beard. His bright green eyes still sparkle, and his front tooth has been missing for years. He still wears his Panama-type hat with a colorful headband. He's still drinking ale, beer, and rum. He's older now but wiser and still a superb musician with his mandolin, piano, and exquisitely beautiful concertina.

As we talked that day, he made a very pertinent comment: "T. Jay, those inboard wells you have in your *Felucca* (intended to accomodate outboard engines) will drown you when you hit a storm at sea! Those waves will be at least thirty feet tall and will come foaming down on you and on the stern of your boat. Those wells will gush water and will sink your boat! You should plug them."

Eventually, I took his good advice and plugged the wells with water baffles (wooden inserts). Ale's suggestion probably saved our lives, considering what happened later, and I was quite pleased to report to him many months later that no water entered through the wells even in the worst conditions we encountered.

We got to our anchorage and spent a hodgepodge schedule of many days scurrying around getting last minute details ready for Our Trip. We shopped for provisions. We went into a drydock and spent a two-day, backbreaking effort for welding and a great deal of cleaning and painting.

After the drydock work, the *Felucca* slid into the water looking ready for anything with her shiny black hull, yellow boot-topping, red storm sail, and off-white mainsails. Our television friends Don and Chuck drove down to make more footage of the *Felucca* as she sailed around San Francisco Bay (my daughter Sean, then sixteen, was aboard that day; we were especially delighted to see her in the television documentary that was shown later).

Two days before our departure I walked into my regular hometown hangout, the *no name bar* in downtown Sausalito, and was lucky enough to run into Spike Africa, the man we knew as the "President of the Pacific Ocean." He was one of Sausalito's best-known residents because of his outgoing nature, his artistic work (macrame and his famous scrimshaw that he carved in his studio over the no name bar), and his overflowing love of life, of adventure, and of sailing. He had a sort of notoriety because of his adventure of sailing to Tahiti with the famous actor Sterling Hayden.

Hayden was in some sort of dispute with his ex-wife and decided to take his four children to sea to get them away from her, and Spike shipped out with him as his first mate. They became fast friends. Spike's wife, Barbara (Red), was the ship's cook, and when they returned from Tahiti, Mr. and Mrs. Africa were charged with conspiracy and child-theft by Hayden's ex-wife (all charges were dismissed by the local district attorney, however).

Although he was born and raised in Ohio, Spike had spent more of his life at sea. Wanderlust had possessed him as a young man and had never left him; he spent more than forty years sailing around most of the world, usually in his preferred wooden sailing ships. He'd been in several employment positions as a sailor or marine expert of some kind throughout his lifetime, and his

Spike Africa,
the "President of the Pacific Ocean"

knowledge of sailing was legendary. Today Spike's sculpted head looks down on you at the no name.

Spike was acting as "host" bartender that day, pouring enormous drinks to all comers. He was wearing his black Greek captain's hat, and his grey bushy eyebrows shaded his piercing, bright blue eyes. His long, greying moustache and goatee matched his eyebrows and helped make him especially noticeable. When I asked him to come with me across the street to the Yacht Club where the *Felucca* was moored, he vaulted across the bar without spilling his drink and said, "Okay, Captain, let's take a look!"

I asked Spike to give me his honest, most candid opinions. Would she make it? Would my homemade rig cross the Pacific safely to Hawaii? Spike was an actor, writer, and sailor. He was Sterling Hayden's first mate about Hayden's 90-foot barkentine *Wanderer* on her sail to Tahiti. Spike's ability as a "hawse pipe" blue-water seaman, scrimshaw expert, and sea storyteller is surpassed by only a few others in this world. I needed some genuine assurance from a man of his experience.

He looked over the *Felucca* while absentmindedly scratching his Vandyke. After what seemed like an eternity, he turned to me and said, "Go on with your cruise, Rockford. She's safe enough to make it."

That was all I needed. I felt, for the first time, that I really would complete Our Trip and many more besides. I never gave another serious thought to those taunts we had received from some of those landlubbers and barside sailors who doubted the *Felucca*'s ability to weather a storm and other adverse conditions at sea. I realized that I was finally and truly ready to leave.

Our last morning for saying good-byes was spent at a mooring off the Sausalito Yacht Club. We exchanged farewells with my mother, my daughter Sean, and many friends before up-anchoring at 3:00 p.m. in the bright afternoon sunlight. As we started to leave, a 26-foot green racing sloop pulled alongside. A gal we know from the sailing club had come to see us off with the owner of the sloop and some friends.

The skipper of another sailing vessel spoke with an incredulous, horrified expression on his face. He gasped, "You're going to Hawaii in *that*?" One last unsolicited you-can't-do-it comment, dammit.

I didn't dignify his comment with a reply, thinking that action speaks louder than words. We hoisted sail and made our dramatic exit immediately. Our red, white, and green jib gave us the colors of an Italian felucca, appropriate perhaps for Fisherman's Wharf or Aquatic Park, so we headed for Aquatic Park to spend our last day on San Francisco Bay.

Halfway across the bay, a black-hulled ketch with white cabin seemed to be after us, overtaking us. I did a "double take" because it was Ann's uncle David Lemon (boat builder, sculptor and sailor) and his girlfriend, Jerry, on the *Nomel*. Dave had built the *Nomel* out of extra scraps from the boatyard where they worked, and it was a beautiful, solid and seaworthy sailing vessel. I quickly adjusted the sails to get the most of the 15 mph wind on our after quarter. The *Felucca* does her best on that slant—I wanted to show Dave close up what a nice sailing vessel she is. Our speed increased with the sail reset and the *Nomel* no longer was overtaking us. Indeed, she was dropping back a bit. Then Dave brought his boat to and hoisted his third sail, the mizzen. With a full press of sails, his beautiful self-designed-and-built 30-foot ketch overtook us. We took photographs for each other, exchanged news and gossip, and said our good-byes.

We dropped anchor in Aquatic Park to make several last minute phone calls, walk around Fisherman's Wharf for a last look for untold days to come, eat ice cream cones and in general bid farewell to the one and only San Francisco. We returned to the boat late in the afternoon and headed for Fort Baker at the northern foot of the Golden Gate Bridge. As we entered the harbor, a modified folk boat named the *Tivoli*—a 26' lapstrak sloop—came alongside. Herb, the skipper, invited us to anchor within Fort Baker Harbor for the night, so we did. Herb was a jet pilot as well as a good sailor, and he came aboard for a gam.

As he left to get back to the *Tivoli*, he said, "Tomorrow when you're out at sea, look for a jet plane. It'll be me, and I'll dive at you. I'll do a couple of rolls as my way of saying good-bye and good luck." And, by gosh, Herb kept his word.

I don't understand how either Ann or I got any rest at all that night, but we tried. The last thing I remember that night was hearing the waves against the hull and seeing the Golden Gate Bridge through the hatch. The next day was to be the first day of Our Trip, a day we'd dreamed of and prepared for for many,

many months. A day I'd prepared for for years, perhaps all my life. When I had finally lived long enough to reach that beautiful clear day out on the Pacific, I had begun to realize that I wasn't merely on another trip, another sojourn that would end at the next port. I had begun to realize that this was my life, and I knew that particular day in my life was one of the most wonderful ones yet.

There have been more of those days since then, and most often, each has been more wonderful than the last.

June 10

I was afraid during the 25 mph winds in the middle of the night that some of those noises I heard meant that some rigging might have given way. I have a habit of using things and not replacing them until they're completely worn out, and that wind last night—with no advance preparation for it—might have done some damage to some of the older rigging. I had brought plenty of rope to renew all tackle and shroud lines but have rigged only one fall aft so far since leaving Sausalito. That was to lift the 250-pound wooden dugout canoe (the *Chiquita*) aboard. I had lashed an 18-foot boom to the bottom of the mizzenmast, attaching the fourfold purchase fall (block and tackle) to the head of the boom. I secured a rope from there to the canoe. So, here I sail with my two-year-old rigging in want of some renewal, and a heavy wind hits unexpectedly. My stinginess in wanting to use the new, excellent Manila hemp rope until it outlasts its strength may bring me trouble someday, but it hasn't yet. And I know I can renew the lines at sea anytime.

About once a month, as a regular task, I go to the top of the mainmast for one reason or another. It's important for me to know that I'm able to fix anything that breaks aboard at sea. I think that if the captain of a sailing vessel can't climb the mast himself then he ought to have a first mate with him who can. I don't really like going up the mast during the voyage.

June 11

There's little wind today. Another turtle came close to the stern; again I missed when I tried to gaff this one. Multitudes of fish swim in the shadow of the boat, keeping pace with our speed day after day. My bait this afternoon was a dark green fish plug; the yellowtails nose it and then turn away. I should know by this time that I am no fisherman.

June 14

The past few days have been sunny and calm with light airs off and on. Progress toward the so-called trade winds is very slow. Three sailors I had spoken with in Puerto Vallarta told me then that the trade winds begin about 600 miles off the coast. We're beyond that mileage and have no northeast wind yet. Our only consolation is that the light air is coming from the north, allowing us to head west. The *Felucca* has been pushed to about 15 degrees latitude, as far south as I want to go. I must head northeast for ten or more days to gain back the 300 or so miles we've lost while drifting south with the current and prevailing breezes. Trade winds, where are you?

Today I peaked the lateens farther vertically than I've yet done. The higher the yards are, the better the boat sails in every way. The last two days were cloudy so I've taken only one noon sight. A breeze came up at 4:00 p.m., blowing all night for a welcome change. It dropped the light airs later today. The boat continues its self-steering, helm tied, so we ought to be able to reach Hawaii without standing any wheel watches!

After playing a couple of chess games, Ann and I dreamed about our house that we would build on Belvedere when we got too old to cruise. The friends I've known the longest time all live in the San Francisco Bay area or in and around my hometown, Healdsburg, California. We discussed the house we wanted in our twilight days, a Mexican-Spanish-style adobe hacienda designed by my architect friend in Puerto Vallarta. We'd put the house on Fitch Mountain, a 999-foot peak I bought nearly thirty-two years ago. It's covered with virgin redwoods, firs, madrone, and oak. It overlooks the Russian River with a 360 degree, 70-mile view of the surrounding five counties. We will rename the mountain "Sotoyome Peak," the original Indian name (from the Pomo Indian chief, Soto, meaning "Soto's home"). I serenaded Ann with my cornet again, played "She's Funny That Way," her favorite, and went to bed early.

We are taking a risk by continuing on at night with both of us asleep. However, it's a calculated risk. We've seen only one freighter so far, and I wonder if any more have passed us while we've slept. We leave our kerosene running lights on at night so that if a ship does come near, they'll see us and warn us by their horns. We hope for the best and expect no trouble from such a meeting if one does, in fact, occur.

June 15

Many people have asked, "Aren't you afraid to go out on the ocean . . . with just you and Ann . . . and that, that . . . *Felucca?*" Though that question was put to me in some form or another many times before we left on this voyage, I still can't answer completely. I'm as afraid of adverse circumstances as any other man, maybe more so. Sometimes I even think Ann has more macho courage than I do; at those times, I hear her saying let's do it or I can do it or something that shows her lack of fear when I'm so scared to death to do it that I just grit my teeth and say, "Well, of course we'll do it. I'll go first." Or some such comment. I go over every detail of the ship, trying to find where there might be some weakness. If there's an unforeseen problem, we could face a calamity from which we might not recover.

So far, we've had more than our share of unforeseen problems. My first rudder was smashed in a gale. The mainsail blew off the mast because of a weak link I hadn't foreseen. The clutch (parrel), a length of one-inch polypropylene rope wrapped around the mast and yard to hold them together, wore out . . . unbeknown to me. The break happened at a dangerous time in a vigorous wind. Since we left Puerto Vallarta, the steering apparatus has broken twice and I've had to go over the side among swarms of fish to do repairs at sea. That scared the hell out of me. A good sailor foresees when a "chink in the armor" might occur and makes repairs before disaster happens. There are enough disasters that sneak up on us unannounced, I think, without my having to encourage their coming.

Last night I thought of another item that needs preventive

maintenance; I'll tend to it tomorrow morning. I need to add a third shroud to the starboard side to give the mast more support in case the other two shrouds break. I'll climb hand over hand to the top of the mast again. That scares me, too, but I'll be more at ease when the job is done. I'm realizing that crossing such a large ocean in such a small craft is frightening all the time. What's the solution? I think it's that I must simply learn to live comfortably with the fear. If anything goes wrong on this boat that I cannot fix, after all, it could mean the end for both of us. We could drift out here for months before anyone ever found us. Or we could simply disappear. And never be heard from again.

There! I've admitted I'm afraid. Now I'll forget it.

Later

God knows I had enough reason to be filled with genuine fear and bone-snapping dread enough times during that voyage. God also knows, however, how that fear and dread got turned into relief and satisfaction in ways *I* never thought about. One time in particular, not too many days prior to those halycon days at the beginning of our voyage from Mexico to Hawaii, we endured a real disaster. We were out of Turtle Bay just three days when we became castaways.

We had enjoyed three glorious days of fine sailing and were heading south toward Baja's Santa Margarita Bay when the weather suddenly turned cloudy, chilly, and foggy. We'd stayed ten to fifteen miles off land and felt completely safe even though we were tired from nonstop sailing. Cabo San Lazaro, a good-sized mountain, had showed up on the horizon about thirty miles away that afternoon before the fog rolled over us; we knew there should be a light on such a prominent point and, since there was very little wind, figured we'd be close by daylight the next morning. As darkness fell, so did the clouds, however, and we were enveloped in a thick, heavy fog. We couldn't see more than a few feet in any direction.

We had no more charged batteries, so the only light we had was our kerosene lamps. We put the tiny trench compass on the settee next to the kerosene lamp there, and the one who was at the wheel would come below occasionally to check the compass.

Now and then the cloud of fog overhead would break and we could check our bearing by the stars, but the compass and the "feel" of the wind on the neck were the main navigational tools we were using. About 10:00 p.m., it was Ann's turn at the watch, and I was thinking that since we were well offshore the wind would stay more or less steady at its gentle speed. We could expect to see the Cabo San Lazaro light within the next two hours, I figured, so I went below and fell into a deep sleep.

I was awakened by Ann's screaming, "T. Jay, come here! Something's wrong! We're in white water!"

I leapt out of bed and shot up on deck. Through the fog I saw phosphorescent water all around the boat. I felt the huge surge of the seas and heard a thunderous crashing of waves on land nearby. I couldn't see the shore but knew we were in a heavy, pounding surf near a beach. The only think I could think of was to stop the boat.

"Hard left!" I yelled to Ann. "We're in the surf!" I was desperately trying to stop forward motion, reversing course so that our anchor could hold us where we were. I ran to the bow and threw over our 40-pound anchor with its twenty-five feet of chain and 200 feet of heavy line. "Oh, God," I thought, "I've lost my *Felucca!*"

The boat turned immediately after the hard left, putting it broadside to the breakers, almost throwing me overboard and putting us in immediate danger of broaching. The moment seemed to last forever although it really happened in only a few seconds. Broaching is a real and terrifying danger not only because it feels like impending death from an erratic and capricious force but also because a broaching boat can lose all control and roll completely over. It will go broadside to the powerful waves, snapping its masts like matchsticks and revolving violently like an egg beater. In surf as high as we were in, a broached boat is lost; most likely, so are its occupants—and we were being forced over on our side with each surge of the waves. Instead of rolling over, however, the *Felucca* gave a dull groan and hit something with a loud thud. I thought we had slammed into the beach. The fog was so heavy that we couldn't see land anywhere and the surf was breaking wildly over the sides.

Suddenly, a gust of wind blew the fog away and we saw that we were pounding sideways on the beach. We glimpsed the low-lying white sand dunes of Magdalena Island. The anchor had dug in but dragged almost uselessly along the sandy bottom. There was nothing we could do to keep the *Felucca* from being washed up to the high watermark on the beach. By this time, simply holding on for dear life and trying to avoid being thrown off the boat into the surf were our only possible courses of action.

We weren't destroyed by broaching, but we were being driven up on the beach. Thank goodness it was a sandy beach and not the more usual beach of jagged rocks! Evidently, the tide was coming in; we were broadside to the tremendous breakers, and each one pushed us a few feet farther up the sand. We had been spared the potential tragedy of rolling over, but we were powerless to stop our inexorable, pulsing movement far up onto the sand. When a boat is driven through the surf onto an exposed ocean shore, there is almost no way to recover the craft. The ocean's breakers defy most attempts at recovery, even with the most powerful of modern devices. There's almost no hope for saving the boat. Certain disaster. Finis. Later, I realized how lucky we really were. Most of the coast we'd passed so far had been nothing but rocks and more sheer, jagged rocks, but this little stretch was beautiful, almost white sand. If we'd been pushed into the coastline anywhere else but on this beach, we would have most certainly been pounded to death on the rocks. With each surge towards higher ground, we were a little safer, just as each surge meant more surely that the *Felucca* would be stranded on the beach, perhaps forever (see photograph, frontispiece). There was nothing else Ann or I could do.

I had a feeling of fatal resignation. So far as I was concerned, Our Trip was ended and the *Felucca* was finished. I had no hope. I'd seen photographs of shipwrecks in books, some of which I had packed for Our Trip, hoping to glean information, advice and counsel from them. One of these pictures came to mind: a 45-foot schooner high and dry on a smooth sandy Atlantic beach near Cape Hatteras, abandoned and given up as lost. I envisioned our ending like that. Our anchor line continued to pull taut after at least an hour of pounding; it brought the bow around so the *Felucca* was pointing out. It kept our bow pointing itself into the crashing breakers instead of sideways to them.

We moved below on the tossing boat into the saloon. We sat opposite each other on the settees. There was nothing to say, and we said nothing. I simply stared into space. We were alive. It looked as if we would survive the debacle, but I felt as if my whole world was crashing down around me. Usually when I'm greatly—or even slightly—perturbed, I'm thrown back to my younger years as an able-bodied seaman. I can curse and swear like the saltiest sea dog, and the cursing helps cover my sometimes despair. At least it's *something* to do. But at that moment I couldn't utter even one four-letter word. I felt like crying but I couldn't cry. My eyes stayed dry. I felt it might be better to be dead.

I finally broke our silence and railed out at Ann. "You—! You've wrecked my boat! It was all I had!" I regretted those words even as they tumbled out of my mouth, and I've regretted them many times since.

Ann is not a woman who sits quietly when someone charges at her stupidly as I was doing. She said for me to do something quite lewd and physically impossible, her eyes flashing. But I knew it wasn't her fault. I knew it then and I know it now. When any ship runs aground and there has to be someone to blame, it's always the captain. No exceptions. We had been in a heavy fog and we were near land, so it was inexcusable for the commander of the vessel to go below, no matter how exhausted I might have been. In a very real way, it was I who had put the *Felucca* on the beach. Not Ann.

The boat kept slamming and pounding in the breakers. She would rise off the sand and then come back down with a shuddering, bone-pounding thud. I discovered later that the ten thousand pounds of rigid concrete ballast developed long cracks about a quarter of an inch wide throughout. The pounding caused the bottom to hog and sag. At least, however, nothing gave way completely. The bulkheads and decks that I'd put on the vessel held. No real material damage occurred other than superficially as we were driven higher and higher up onto the beach. Because the *Felucca* started life as a standard 35-foot ship's lifeboat, she stood almost straight up on the sand throughout it all. Almost erect. Her slightly V-shaped bottom and wide beam were like a cargo ship which, when grounded in the sand, will stay almost upright. Her own basic characteristics saved her from serious damage.

I apologized to Ann as best I could, and I asked her what had happened. She was just as distressed as I was, and she assured me she understood the real reasons behind my stupid outburst.

"You know, T. Jay, how overcast and foggy it is. I couldn't see the stars to steer by and just went below to check the compass. I lashed the wheel and went below about fifteen minutes. When I went back up, I saw the white water and shouted for you," she explained. She was about as miserable as I was. At least she was also beyond the point where tears would help.

Ann wears a hearing aid because her hearing is about forty-five percent of normal. She didn't hear the breakers. When she lashed the wheel, the breaking combers weren't very close. When she went below, the current caught the boat and began pulling it rapidly toward the shore. Below deck, within the double-walled construction in the saloon where the compass is, the sound of the surf simply didn't come through to her. We tried our best to comfort each other, and I tried to tell her how much I wanted to take back the terrible things I'd just told her.

Later, we found out that this was one of the most treacherous shores on the entire Mexican coast. The current runs directly east toward this beach at three miles per hour. For years, large ships have been running aground on this very beach. A chart I saw a short time afterwards indicated three wrecks of full-sized merchant ships. Two of them, we discovered, were still visible on the beach. We also found out afterward that the Cabo San Lazaro light we'd been looking for was out of order. A combination of bad luck and laxity on my part had brought us to this end.

Even after we were obviously stuck in the place we would stay, perhaps forever, the continuous pounding continued. It accentuated my distress even further. I couldn't stand feeling and hearing those pounding waves against my beached boat any longer and took the double sleeping bag out onto the sand. I wanted to avoid hearing the obvious. And I needed rest.

"Are you coming with me?" I asked Ann.

"No, T. Jay, you go ashore. I'll stay with the *Felucca*," she replied with great sadness.

By this time the water was only about two feet deep in the lesser surges. I climbed down the boarding ladder and Ann threw me the sleeping bag. I slowly trudged up the beach to the top of the huge sand dune that overlooked the pounding, floundering *Felucca*. The sky had begun to clear, and the moon showed through in the clear spots to illuminate the *Felucca* in her struggle to survive in the crashing surf. I found a high, dry spot, took

61

off my wet, dripping pants and got into the mercifully dry sleeping bag. I fell into a deep, unconscious sleep.

I awakened the next morning well after sunrise. The tide was out, and the boat was high and dry and silent. It was still sitting upright. Throwing open the sleeping bag, reaching for my pants, I noticed what looked like many large fresh dog tracks around me in the sand. Dogs on the beach? On *this* beach? Peering one way and then the other, I caught a glimpse of what looked like mangy police dogs. They weren't police dogs. They were coyotes!

Looking more carefully, I saw five or six of them slinking around through the sand dunes. I shuddered slightly with a sinking feeling in my stomach, thinking how grateful I was that they didn't devour me in the night. I thought I'd read somewhere, however, that coyotes don't molest a human being unless the person has been incapacitated and is lying quite still for some time. I tried hard to believe that was the truth about coyotes, anyway. They seemed curious about me and kept trying to get closer. Were they hungry?

As quickly as I could, I went down the huge sand dunes and got back to the boat. I knew the boat would get me high enough above them to be safe. I got some bread and threw them some. That was it. Six of them hesitantly overcame their distrust of me and worked their way cautiously towards the bread, grabbing it and running a good distance away from me to eat. After several days of this sort of thing, they became almost friendly, mincing in their stiff-legged gait to within thirty yards of the boat and, at night, coming to within a few feet to eat the scraps we threw over for them.

That first morning, however, the coyotes were not my primary concern. I needed to find some help. Looking north from our position on Coyote Beach, I could see a long, flat sand beach backed by low dunes. In the opposite direction, I could see what had to be the "out of order" light location on Cabo San Lazaro, about fifteen miles away. I walked at least two miles inland over the sand dunes to the top of the tallest hillock to try to see some sign of civilization in the valley beyond. Turning west, I could see the *Felucca* standing in the white surf, her pennants and flags flying from mast and yards—a melancholy sight. I could see at least thirty miles, thirty miles of nothing. There was no sign whatsoever of anybody else or anything anywhere. I trudged back to the boat.

Ann and I had to decide what to do next. We had to get help, even though it seemed to me that nothing could take us off the beach. Ann stubbornly clung to her opinion that we could be pulled off the beach, through the pounding surf, if we could get a big enough ship to pull us. I was convinced we were there to stay, but Ann's optimism helped change my mind. Anything is possible, I conceded. We deliberated over a huge, delicious breakfast and decided to walk south along the beach toward Cabo San Lazaro; if we found something along the way, well and good, and then we'd not have to go all the way. We dressed for hiking and filled our backpacks with sweaters, sandwiches, and water. I also took my two-foot telescope, and at about 8:30 a.m. we started walking along the flat, wet Pacific coast. We enjoyed the beauty of the flat, wet coastline in spite of the impetus for the walk that the *Felucca* had given us.

After our first four hours we were footsore and muscle-weary from walking. We were sailors, not walkers. We hadn't walked any real distance in a long time, and the last time we'd walked at all was in Ensenada. All along the shore was evidence of wooden shipwrecks from years ago. Skeletons of old ship parts stuck out of the sand every few miles. No wonder this area had such a bad reputation as a ship's graveyard! And all kinds of flotsam and jetsam—bottles, shoes, driftwood, dead fish, shells, and white bones—littered the beach. All broken and useless things get thrown up on the shore, we said to each other, including our *Felucca*. We felt sick inside.

About ten miles south of the *Felucca* we came upon a shipwrecked freighter. She was sitting upright, parallel to the sea. The similarity of her position to the *Felucca's* was a sobering one. She'd been gutted and stripped by torches when someone salvaged all of her equipment and metals that had any value, and it was now no more than a 400-foot empty rusting hulk lying on this twenty-five-mile beach of wrecked ships. We tried to rest each hour, but the sights of so many unfortunate vessels that had met their end on this lonely strip of beach was a sharp reminder of what fate probably had in mind for ours, too. We trudged on, and by 1:00 p.m., we were no more than halfway to Cabo San Lazaro. It was clear that I'd miscalculated on the distance; our boat was at least twenty-five miles from the point.

We routed countless coyotes along the way, shooing them from their meals of rotting porpoises, fish, and dead seabirds as we passed. I'd never *seen* so many coyotes. I was raised in Lake County, California, and had seen coyotes there all my life, but never so many as here. I tried whistling to them and some would respond by pricking up their ears and looking around for the source of the whistle. Then they'd lope off in that peculiar stiff-legged trot with heads lowered, and they'd slink off out of our way to hide behind the sand dunes until we passed.

As we neared the cape in the afternoon, a huge, completely intact freighter showed up, lodged on the rocks in the corner of a small inlet. It had not been there very long, obviously, and there was a guard aboard to watch her! But he had no radio—no resources to help us—and all he could do was direct us to continue our trek southward. This entire stretch of beach was positively a magnet for drawing ships to their doom!

By late afternoon, we reached the tree-lined bayou that leads to Santa Margarita Bay. It was only a few more miles to civilization. From a small rise, we caught sight of two sailing boats at anchor well offshore. We tried to reach them by shouting, but the noise of the surf kept our voices from being heard by any of those who were on the vessels that were sailing merrily past just offshore. We weren't far from Cabo San Lazaro now, and we realized we had to keep walking; the sailors on the boats we saw couldn't hear us.

I could tell that Ann's feet hurt considerably. I insisted that she wait for me to go on and return for her, but she gamely insisted on keeping pace and insisted that we continue together. She would not stay. Then, without warning, we came upon a crude fishing camp. We discovered several open fishing boats, a lean-to building with three makeshift beds inside and cooking equipment with rice and beans still warm on the outdoor stove. The place was deserted. As we made bad jokes about Goldilocks, we ate some of the food. We made more bad jokes and lay down on the beds to rest.

No sooner than we had laid down, the sound of a boat motor announced the arrival of three men. They were extremely curious about who these people were who were eating their food and resting in their beds, but they seemed very friendly. They smiled and tried to communicate the best they could; they spoke little or no English, and we spoke precious little Spanish. We learned that Senor Ray was the bossman, but we learned little else about the men. We drew pictures and made several charade efforts, and in a short time the men came to understand that we were castaways who needed help.

The fishermen kindly took pity on us and motored us back, in their large skiff with powerful outboard motor, out of the bayou into the bay to the anchored cruising yachts. To our great amazement, two young sailors we had met in Ensenada put their heads out of the cabin of their 35-foot sloop. Tom and Paul were two young men who were heading down to Panama and had anchored here to take a short break from sailing. I say they were "young"; they were only about twenty-one or twenty-two, but they were both quite strong, and I had earlier seen that they were quite good sailors. It gave me a good feeling to see them.

"Hi, T. Jay! Hi, Ann! What the hell are you doing here? Did you guys *walk*? Where's the *Felucca*?" It didn't take them long to understand that we weren't out walking for pleasure, and we told them our tale of woe. They fed us well and invited us to stay the night. We were elated to find someone we actually knew here in this ship's graveyard, and their warm hospitality was like a magic elixir for our spirits. The boys used our appearance as an excuse, they said, to open a bottle of precious spirits, and we all four got slightly tipsy enjoying it after dinner. I don't think they really needed an excuse; Ann and I certainly didn't after all that had happened.

The next morning we made specific plans. Tom and Paul accepted my offer of $50 cash to help us by finding a large ship or fishing boat to pull us off the beach—or the same amount quadrupled to them directly if they could pull us off with their schooner by herself. I couldn't bring myself to believe that the schooner's engine, by itself, could succeed at the effort to free the *Felucca*, but I was as ready as the other men were to try.

Tom and Paul accepted the challenge with elan and enthusiasm. One of them got on the ship's radio and made a number of general distress calls for help. He broadcast the offer of U.S. $200 cash to any skipper of a boat large enough to come to "Coyote Beach" and pull the *Felucca* off at high tide. And of course they were determined to try to earn the $200 themselves by using their own boat. We up anchored at the first chance that morning and hurried through the mouth of Santa Margarita Bay toward

65

the *Felucca* under full sail with the engine at full power, assisting the wind.

Their rescue of our boat this way was not to be. Four miles off land, their steering apparatus collapsed, and we spent the rest of the day and all that night simply getting safely back into the bay. Was I bad luck? Their rudder failed, too! We tried several tricks to make up for the rudder loss, but nothing worked. We finally resorted to the ultimate insult to the schooner by towing her with their little skiff with its 3 ½-horsepower Seagull engine. We anchored back near the same spot from which we had left in such high spirits earlier that same morning; in the middle of the night, our spirits were at a new low. Even so, I thanked God we made it back without beaching.

The next morning, Ann and I took their skiff over to the other boat anchored nearby. It was a larger fishing boat with Mexican registration. I could see quickly that this boat seemed to have the shape and engine power to be a likely candidate for our successful tow, but once again I was handicapped as monolingual. At least this time there were charts to point to. With broad pantomime and pigeon Spanish, we managed to get the main facts across to the skipper. He agreed to come and pull us off the beach!

But he spoke numbers in English well enough to make it clear that $200 was not acceptable; he insisted on $500.

I pleaded, in my best Spanish, "Me pobrecito gringo. No mucho dinero. Por favor, Captain."

He smiled broadly and answered in Spanish. I didn't understand a word. It was clear, however, that our interview was at an end and that it was time to leave. The skipper surprised us by proffering us generous amounts of freshly caught shrimp, lobster, and flounder—which, of course, we were happy to take. There was a live, three-foot-wide turtle on its back on deck with its head thrown back, mouth open, and blood dripping from its mouth. It was churning its feet and head in protest. After giving us the other seafood, the skipper pointed to the turtle, indicating that he wanted us to take some of it. I nodded yes. I'd had turtle stew at Gordo's and knew what a delicacy it was.

The skipper ordered one of the men to cut the turtle into pieces. The man drew a large, long knife out of his hip scabbard and deftly cut the helpless turtle out of its shell. I've seldom seen such an appalling sight. Ann turned her head in horror, but I watched in fascination. Even as the fisherman cut the turtle from its shell it was still bleeding and moving convulsively. Only when it was completely out did it finally die. The skipper gave us five pounds of the fine pink meat, and we tried to look and act grateful. Both of us were trying to smile and not to vomit as we accepted the dripping turtle meat.

We returned to the schooner and split the food with Tom and Paul, 50-50. They motored us up the bayou to the fishing camp, and we resumed our fractured conversations with the bossman, Senor Ray. He had a pickup truck, he said, an old Chevy, and yes, he would drive us the twenty-five miles back up the beach to the *Felucca*. He agreed to accept some gasoline and a portable radio for his help. The bargain was well worth the loss of our radio, since neither Ann nor I felt able to make the return by foot, especially not with our arms full of fresh, heavy seafood.

We got to the *Felucca* after about an hour of driving. It was low tide, and she was in the same position we'd left her in. She was still whole except for some damage that was visible on the rudder; the continuous slamming of the surf during high tide had begun its destruction. I gave the truck driver five gallons of gasoline and our inexpensive radio/record player. I asked him please to return in three days, saying I'd give him more gasoline and another gift. He smiled, shook his head violently in the affirmative, and drove away waving broadly. Ann and I put the seafood away and went to bed immediately, sleeping like the dead in spite of the increasing pounding that the incoming tide was causing.

We woke the next morning feeling more rested than we had in a few days. I decided to try to kedge—to move the boat with anchor and line—into the surf at high tide. Kedging off the beach is an exercise that most sailors must do with their sailing vessel from time to time if they are sailing extensively in strange waters. If one has taken the ground as we had, one of the methods to try is to take the anchor, secured to the stem of the grounded boat, and row out to set it into deeper water. While returning to the boat in the skiff, vigorous pulls on the anchor line will often drag the vessel into deeper water off the shallow spot on which she had grounded.

In our case, we needed to kedge the *Felucca* in a forward direction out into the deeper surf so that when she reached deep enough water to float she could catch the right winds and sail away to freedom. If and when a ship showed up, I'd be all ready to be pulled off the beach. I ran a 200-foot line on the 25-pound anchor out into the surf ahead of the boat at low tide. At high tide I was then able to move her farther into the water until she was afloat. We used block and tackle, pulling her out fifteen feet at a time before resetting the tackle.

We spent several backbreaking hours just moving the boat 100 feet. When she got to the floating point, however, she began plunging violently in the rolling surf. Even then, we continued pulling, hoping that if we could survive the beating by the next tide—and trying to help by running the line out another thirty feet—we'd be able to get her past the first big breaker. Yes, we sort of knew it was impossible, but we had to try, nevertheless.

It *was* impossible. The boat groaned and yawed sideways to the surf, bounding around like an hysterical elephant. In one of these jerking, lurching rolls, Ann was thrown free off the deck, through the air and into the pounding surf. I didn't see her go but, fortunately, I heard her cries for help. I quickly looked for her but couldn't see her anywhere. She called again, and I knew I was looking on the wrong side of the boat. I leapt to the other side and saw her head in the foaming white water. She was screaming, "The ladder! The ladder!"

I grabbed the boarding ladder and put it down the side so she could try to scramble aboard. In the meantime, the *Felucca* was constantly being driven broadside to the onrushing breakers. Ann was in between them and the iron hull of the boat. For a moment, I felt the terror of realizing that the heavy surf could easily pound her to a pulp against the boat! At that moment, a huge surge of water pushed her towards the boat just high enough for me to grab her. I reached down and grabbed her upraised arm by her wrist and pulled upwards with all my strength. I don't think I could have brought her aboard if she hadn't had the good sense to use her free arms to reach for the ladder, grab it and pull her feet onto the rungs, pushing upwards as I pulled.

Together, we got her back on board. My gratitude for her safety was a physical feeling. I had a few moments of profound fear until we were reassured that she was not injured. She suffered a genuine personal loss because her hearing aid and her glasses had both been lost in the waves. For the rest of the trip, she had to function in that special kind of discomfort that only those who need such devices can truly understand. I was grateful that she was alive and uninjured.

When the tide came in and pushed us back to our original position on the beach, I finally admitted that it was impossible to kedge in such a mighty surf. A large, powerful engine in a large vessel was the only thing that would pull the *Felucca* off this beach and clear her from this surf. At the highest point of the tide, I was at my lowest ebb of the trip. I'd given up any idea of getting off this beach without a miracle. The only miracle I could imagine was a ship large enough to tow us off. But in our state of low finances, it would be impossible to pay for such assistance from anybody. I was convinced that the *Felucca* was there to stay, and Ann and I began to discuss how we would continue at least the part of Our Trip that would involve our exploring Mexico. We talked about how we would walk every step of the way with packs on our backs. I was determined to continue in spite of our terrible misfortune. So we discussed what we saw our options to be:

(1) We could dismantle the boat, taking out the usable, moveable parts (blocks, ropes, masts, sails, and the like) and have our Mexican friend in his truck carry them to the nearest village. We could then buy another hull and build the *Frisco Felucca III* along the same general plan as the beloved *Felucca* we had just lost. Or we could (2) sell all our equipment and valuables too heavy to carry and buy two bicycles. We could make two small trailers with bicycle wheels on them in order to carry our camping and living gear behind us. This way we could travel through Mexico and Central America. We could get at least to Panama on bicycles with small trailers, we thought.

Or we could (3) still make the trip on foot. This would be our least expensive option, and we could use backpacks and pull carts like the Mormons used in the early nineteenth century when they were moving west to Salt Lake City. I'd seen pictures of large-wheeled pull carts which they pulled behind themselves, walking between the shafts as horses pull a wagon. These carts had covered wagon tops shaped like a horseshoe. I planned the platform of each cart to be three by four feet, two feet deep, with bicycle wheels and the "covered wagon" top.

Ann and I discussed these possibilities at length. Our discussion of each was enthusiastic at first and then, as we got more and more deeply involved in the details of "what we were gonna do," we got less enthusiastic. The discussions helped keep us from being totally devastated emotionally. After all, we had sailed victoriously down the coast of California and Baja California this far . . . and here we were, castaways on a deserted beach in Mexico. Yes, we were down. But we were not *out*.

The next day, no one appeared. Our miracle did not occur. No boats, no trucks, no pedestrians, no other castaways. I consoled myself with future plans, but I was feeling more and more bleak and desolate. Ann gathered driftwood from the beach and sand dunes so that we'd have plenty of firewood for our Yukon stove. At noon the following day, however, things began to change.

I heard an unusual noise, looked up, and we saw our friend Ray in his pickup. He was tooting his horn as he drove over as near to us as he could get. I had written two letters that I wanted him to deliver—one to the naval base on Santa Margarita Island and the other to the boys in the schooner. I was thrilled to see Senor Ray again and invited him and his two friends aboard. I reached into the clothes closet, pulled out my lightweight shadow-plaid sport jacket and asked Ray to put it on. His eyes sparkled with delight. His clothes were ragged. His tennis shoes belonged on smaller feet; the toes were cut out so that he could get them on. I was right in thinking that he'd appreciate some nice clothes. He was the same size as I, and my jacket fit him perfectly. I didn't have to adjust the coat any more than a smoothing hand here, a smart tuck there; it quickly fit as well across the shoulders as if it had been tailored especially for Senor Ray.

I said, "You like? It's yours! It is for you." And I gave him five gallons of gasoline when I asked him if he would deliver our messages. As I had hoped, Senor delivered the messages.

Two days later everyone showed up! Senor Ray and company came tooting and roaring down the beach. A Mexican fishing vessel snorted its horn and dropped anchor about a half mile offshore from us. The boys in the schooner anchored nearby. And, to the surprise and pleasure of all of us, I think, a minesweeper from the Mexican Navy circled and dropped anchor near the other two boats! The Navy vessel made an impressive sight; it was splashed with brilliant red and green with white on her mast-head, the number 16 was emblazoned in huge numerals on her bow next to her name, the *Dragaminas*, and her flags and pennants announced her official importance in ways visible from miles away. We had rescuers standing in line.

When Ann asked me, "What do you think, now, T. Jay?" I blurted out that I thought it looked like the second coming of Jesus. It was like an armada! Perhaps the two smaller vessels together could have gotten the *Felucca* back in the water, but it was obvious that the Mexican Navy vessel could do it by herself.

Quickly, we began making final preparations for being hauled off the shore at high tide. We had to kedge the boat ourselves with our own equipment to the point of almost floating at high tide, attaching 1,000 yards of 3-inch hawser from the Navy ship through the heavy surf so that we could tie it on our vessel and give the signal to heave. As we were doing that, the captain of the *Dragaminas 16* sent us a gift package of canned meats and coffee. The fishermen didn't stay to see the end of the saga they'd seen begin, but before they left they sent us a plastic laundry bag full of freshly caught and cooked shrimp with several fresh limes in the bag. Tom and Paul were the deliverymen for these gifts, rowing the food through the surf, and they joined Ann and me aboard that evening for a wonderfully special shrimp dinner. Our spirits had quickly risen to the point where we were ecstatic.

After the few days of deep discouragement, disappointment, or whatever you want to call it, we were feeling especially buoyant with such good prospects to save the *Felucca*. After dinner that night, we finished off the last of our meager liquor supply, and I stood on deck, watching the surf and the Mexican Navy. I took a deep breath and held it. When I exhaled, I felt as though an enormous weight had been lifted from my shoulders. I had never before believed in miracles. Since that breath, I have believed.

The tide was high enough by noon the next day. With the help of our two young friends, Tom and Paul, the Navy's hawser was secured to stemhead and mast. The skipper asked the young men to give a signal when we were ready to be pulled, and at the proper moment they took off in their wet suits and worked their skiff to the Navy vessel to give this word: "When Captain Rockford feels all is ready, he will signal you on his cornet. Then you are, please, to pull." I stood on the deck of the *Felucca* watching

Tom and Paul as they spoke with the Mexican skipper; he was standing with several officers, and they were all watching us with binoculars. It hit me as a very melodramatic moment, and these lines rushed into my memory:

> . . . He signaled to the pitcher,
> and bade the game go on. . . . .

I don't know why "Casey at the Bat" came to mind, but as it did I brought my cornet to my lips and played Louis Armstrong's introduction to "West End Blues." When the skipper of the Navy vessel heard that and saw our hand signals, his ship began to move forward, away from us and out to sea. The hawser tightened through the high tide waters that surrounded the *Felucca*. There was no great noise, no giant thrust, no special anything. We simply moved. Slowly, to be sure, but we moved. For several moments, I refused to believe that it was working, but it was obvious that we were moving foot by foot out into deeper water. We were slowly moving through the shallow, sand-filled water toward the huge breakers; the breakers began to pound as mercilessly as before, but this time they did not push us back on the beach! The rescue effort was working!

"But screw your courage to the sticking point and you'll not fail," quoted Ann. She had the most uncanny ability of quoting some particularly appropriate quotation from somewhere at just the right moment.

"You'd better believe it," I answered.

As the *Felucca* moved at a snail's pace out past her total depth draw (2¾ feet), we picked up speed. It was increasingly clear that we had a very good chance of getting out. I drew a big breath, gritted my teeth, clenched my jaw, and here came Casey again:

> . . . They saw his face grow cold and stern;
> they saw his muscles strain . . . .

We stood on deck watching hypnotically as our boat cut through the smaller first breakers. We had a four-foot freeboard over the water level, so I didn't expect any trouble until we got to the higher waves, the "monster waves" that Ann was looking at with such trepidation. But now the minesweeper was pulling a little faster; the *Felucca* would climb one gigantic swell and then bury her nose almost completely under the larger oncoming, foaming breaker. It seemed like only moments before we were on top of the first of those last murderous waves.

. . . Strike one, the umpire said . . . .

We rode the first huge wave like a roller coaster, up at a firm slow speed and then down as if we were falling. We hit the bottom of the ride with a wet, splashy thud and started our ascent up the second breaker. This time, we rode upwards at a sharper angle and dug in at the bow more than on the first wave, and then we submarined under the surface down its back, almost buying the total freeboard at the bow. I heard a ripping, wood-breaking noise as part of the wooden bulkhead gave way at the bow.

. . . That ain't my style, cried Casey. Strike two, the umpire said . . . .

We were taking water inside through the broken part of the bow because of that underwater trip down the second huge wave. We were also taking heavy seas over the bow. Up to this point, even in winds up to 50 mph speeds we'd been in already. I hadn't seen the *Felucca* take on water on deck no matter if we were going downwind or hove to or at sea anchor. Her high freeboard made her an especially dry cruiser, but we were taking on water by the tubful.

. . . And then the air was shattered by the force of Casey's blow . . . .

There was just this last monster breaker to get through alive and in one piece. It was the biggest one. While we were low beneath it we could see nothing else but its curving underbelly, all slick and green with a frothing, snow white overhanging crest whose white spume was blowing off toward the shore. Thinking back about it, I think it looked a lot like we were the surfer in one of those surfing pictures of the ultimate surfer's wave. It

certainly wasn't simply an exciting challenge for us; it was a genuine threat to our survival. The *Felucca*'s nose was down and plowing into the bottom of this huge wave; she was fighting desperately to rise up over this wave and not bury herself. We were at the back end of the boat, scared and hanging on for dear life. For a split second, it looked as if the sea might win and take her, but she gave such a lunge that I was nearly swept off my feet. She pushed her bow almost straight up so quickly that the water's crashing away made a loud noise. She came up, up, and up until she was stable at about a 45-degree angle. She seemed to be practically standing on her stern. Then we neared the top of the wave and nosed right through to the other side and immediately submarined, going underwater all the way down the backside of the biggest wave I think I'd ever seen. My relief was visceral when we shot out of the water clear of the surf!

We were free and out on the open Pacific again! By the grace of God and the help of the Mexican Navy we had a second chance to continue Our Trip aboard the *Frisco Felucca II.*

. . . There was ultimate joy aboard that night.
The *Felucca* did *not* strike out!

After it was apparent to everyone that we were safely clear of the formidable breakers, the minesweeper's ship-to-shore boat came alongside us with the executive officer in command. He looked quite dashing in his full khaki uniform with a spate of colorful medals, and he announced quite formally, "The captain of *Dragaminas 16* invites the skipper and first mate of the *Frisco Felucca* aboard as his guests. We will put three men aboard your vessel. The captain asks you to have dinner and stay overnight for the trip into Santa Margarita Bay." The officer was continuing what was to become a lengthy period of gentlemanly and discerning behavior from the Mexican Navy personnel toward us. He indicated that we'd be anchoring for the night in the bay and then proceeding next morning to the naval base. Of course, I accepted the invitation.

Soon enough, we were aboard the minesweeper. The skipper came down from the bridge, bowed smartly to us and introduced himself as Captain Jaime Perez-Elias. He and I only shook hands but Ann hugged him and kissed him on the cheek; he hugged back vigorously, she told me later, and he warmly welcomed us aboard. He's a tall slim man in his late thirties, Spanish background evident in his aquiline nose, light complexion, and gracefully erect carriage. He was wearing his captain's hat and looked especially good in uniform. There's no question that this man is the captain of not only the ship but of everything around him. His men obviously respect and adore him. When Captain Jaime smiles or laughs, everyone else around him does the same—not because they feel they ought to but because his cheer is genuinely infectious. Somehow, however, he seems to retain his dignity no matter what. Even though one may feel sometimes like clapping him heartily on the back, one would not dare. After all, he is the distinguished captain.

Captain Jaime led us topside to the officer's saloon and told us there was a guest stateroom prepared for us if we'd like to retire, and then he asked us to join him for lunch at 2:00 p.m. Our first crew member who served as a helper for us established a standard of civility and friendliness that was constantly equalled and sometimes surpassed by each other crew member with whom we had contact aboard this ship. Captain Jaime's entire crew did all that they could possibly do to make us feel comfortable. The jolly first engineer, Rubin, even invited me to his cabin for a chat and a glass of mescal (incidentally, I discovered that mescal is one Mexican hard liquor with a punch roughly equal to a few sticks of dynamite).

As we were being royally treated, the *Dragaminas 16* was moving south at an appropriately slow speed, happily towing the *Felucca* five hundred feet behind. During a delightful lunch, Captain Jaime explained that his ship was one of the Mexican Naval vessels that was assigned to accompany a sailboat race from San Diego to Puerto Vallarta, and his orders included the directive "to aid and assist any sailing vessels along that pathway during the race." He had received special orders from Mexico City by ship's telegraph to proceed from his earlier position at sea in order to look for us and try to rescue us from "shipwreck beach." Evidently our handwritten message to the naval base a few days earlier was wired to Mexico City and then to the minesweeper which was already near us at the time. Whatever the actual details were, they certainly made for fortunate circumstances for us.

T. J. R.
Bangkok, Thailand
April 1, 1974

In the evening after supper and the lengthy conversation period with the officers afterward, we retired to our stateroom. The only thing missing that would complete the red-carpet treatment was a mint on the pillow! Ruben had even had the ordinarily cold bathing water heated so that Ann could take a hot shower. We were treated like royalty.

Shortly after sunup, the ship neared the naval base. When we arrived, the minesweeper dropped the hook and pulled the *Felucca* alongside so that we could reboard. As we did so, the entire ship's company lined at attention on the foredeck. The captain and chaplain stood nearby, and all of them suddenly bowed their heads. We could hear the chaplain's prayer, and we were surprised to hear the name, *Frisco Felucca*, mentioned several times. Ann and I were in our most prayerful-looking positions, and we whispered our thoughts that they were saying their Sunday prayers that included talking about the rescue and thanking the Almighty for their success.

After we boarded her, the *Felucca* was pulled alongside a small working dock at the base. We disembarked and walked to the base headquarters where we met the admiral and rear admiral. Both were unusually kind and both were gentlemen of the highest rank. Before we finally left the base, both came aboard the *Felucca*, signed our logbook and helped us drink a goodly supply of our coffee. They were quite curious about our "character" boat and inspected every inch they could. They frequently commented on how they had "saved" this "interesting" and "charming" boat from extinction, and they seemed to grow increasingly proud that they had done so. Shortly before they left, they had offered us full access to *all* of the services they had at the base!

Within an hour after the admiral and rear admiral left us, a team of five workmen arrived. They were carrying welding equipment, tools, mechanical devices, boxes, carts—they looked as if they were prepared to perform a complete mechanical makeover. For the first time, I began to feel a little queasy. This was *Sunday*, for Pete's sake; nobody works on Sunday. If they do, they charge much, much more than they ordinarily charge. My mind began to reel at the size of the payoff eventually required because of all this Sunday work. Ann reassured me that we would find some way to pay the bill, that the work was truly needed and that we could relax. After all, the workmen didn't seem as if they were bothered by working on Sunday. They were as cheerful as if they had been members of Captain Jaime's crew aboard the *Dragaminas 16*, and they each seemed genuinely interested in every detail of the *Felucca*. Ann's confidence helped me to avoid biting my nails or worrying too deeply about the exorbitant costs we might face, and the good and positive events within this part of the Mexican Navy continued; our handsome, well-tailored Captain Jaime appeared.

Captain Jaime just wanted to say hello and check to see that work had begun. When we began to question how we would pay for the repairs, he said that we had no need to worry about paying. I had calculated and recalculated such things as towing charge, overnight stateroom and service, five workmen at triple time on Sunday . . . . But Captain Jaime said we had no need to worry. I couldn't believe him, so I worried nonetheless.

He volunteered to send a telegram for us, and we each sent one to our respective parents to ask for money. Then he asked if we had money for food and supplies. Our protestations must not have been convincing, because he ordered the base grocery store opened for us so that we could get some necessary supplies. And he pulled out his wallet, took out several U.S. twenty dollar bills, and handed me two of them.

"Here, take this. Pay me back when you can. Fifty days or fifty years. Whatever you wish," he said with a smile that confirmed his words and elevated the gesture into the realm of gentlemanly behavior of the finest order. Ann and I were deeply impressed and touched. If I could have let myself do what Ann did, I would have gotten teary-eyed, too; she hugged and kissed Captain Jaime with genuine gusto.

And then the base's doctor visited us aboard. He was as fascinated by the *Felucca* as the others, and we went through the full inspection tour one more time. He was an energetic and charming man, and he noticed the Ojotone fish that had not much more time before it would be better seagull food than people food. With a twinkle in his eye, he told us that he was a gourmet cook and he kept glancing at the fish as he spoke.

I picked up his broad hint and asked, "How would you prepare this fish?"

He immediately invited himself to cook, serve, and help eat our next meal, and Ann introduced him to our galley. The good doctor cleaned and, true to his word, served and helped us eat some of the most deliciously prepared fish we'd had in a long time. We pored over his work as he prepared the fish and saw that his culinary trick was to cut diagonal slashes on both sides of the filleted fish, rub a palmful of salt into the incisions, and then simmer fifteen minutes in bubbling hot oil. "Muy sabrosa," indeed.

After dinner, late in the evening, I went to a movie with the rear admiral and walked to his quarters for a nightcap afterwards. We enjoyed a boisterous conversation about this and that and, as I was leaving, he insisted that I take back to Ann several cans of cold beer and two enormous lobsters. As if Ann weren't totally charmed enough by these men already!

The next day, after all repairs had been completed, Captain Jaime appeared. He seemed pleased over the progress of his workmen, and asked, "What time would be satisfactory for you to leave if I can get official clearance to tow you out of the bay?"

I couldn't believe it. A *captain* standing there, asking *me* what time it would be convenient to do *me* a favor and tow us out to sea! I said something like, "Anytime that's convenient for you, sir, will most certainly be convenient for me."

Ann and I expressed our heartfelt thanks to Captain Jaime for his kindnesses, his hospitality, and his generosity. Of course, Ann hugged and kissed him good-bye. And she wouldn't let us leave until she had gone to the officers' headquarters and hugged and kissed the admirals good-bye, too. They all seemed to love this attention and treated it as very "old world" and appropriate. As things developed, 3:00 p.m. was the most "convenient" time, and by then we were again under tow behind the *Dragaminas 16*, heading this time out to the open Pacific, once again moving south on Our Trip.

Everything connected with our contact with the Mexican Navy seemed to have happened so *quickly*. One moment, we were marooned on a beach. Castaways with little hope. Then we were rescued and treated like a king and queen. Now we were flush with gifts and wonderful memories of charming people and friendly helpers, and here we were resuming Our Trip with a beautifully repaired *Felucca*. All this, and we were charged *nothing*! No one would even hear of our promise to pay. Each time I asked, "How much do I owe you," everyone from admiral to captain to worker kept saying, "Nada." Nothing. No charge. I had trouble believing my own ears, even as they kept hearing the same thing. The entire experience seemed like something out of a fairy tale. I said that to Ann and she reminded me that she always did believe in fairy tales. I never did, but, after our experience with the Mexican Navy, I do now.

As we were being towed out from the base, the Navy Drum and Bugle Corps stood at attention on the parade ground adjacent to the bay. I could easily see them and tried to single out individual faces with my "scope." Trumpets and drums played a ceremonial call, and rifle shots echoed from many rifles with the noise bouncing back and forth off the nearby sand dunes. There was nothing else I could think of doing but answering with my battered old 1905 Kohler & Chase horn. I raised it when the Corps was finished and blew solid fortissimo—the military bugle call, "To the Colors"—my parting salute to the Mexican Navy.

About two hours later, we were at the mouth of the bay. About four miles offshore I raised the sails and tossed free the towline. At long last, the *Felucca* took wing again. The crew of the *Dragaminas 16* once again lined her railings as she circled us, and this time many of the men were taking pictures. This was the first time they'd seen her with sails and colors flying, and they waved and shouted with upraised arms and thumbs up. She circled once more and then headed south into the ocean. Slowly the *Dragaminas 16* disappeared in the distance. As the minesweeper was still in view, I made myself a solemn promise with Ann's listening: "Never again, while I'm in command of a vessel at sea, will I directly or indirectly head towards land when my exact position is unknown or visibility is poor." I elaborated further: "Under these circumstances I will head by compass course into the opposite direction of where I believe land to be." The solemnity of my promise helped some, but I still felt the guilt for a long time.

Seldom is a man given a second chance like I was. I was grateful for that chance and fully intended to benefit from what I'd learned from our harrowing experience of a shipwreck on Coyote Beach. With one last glimpse of the *Dragaminas 16* on the horizon, I threw them one last, "Thank-you," and put the entire episode from my mind. The world was again my oyster, and Our Trip was under way once again.

June 17—450 miles out, sailed unseeing through five islands

For the past ten days we've been in very light air, no stronger than 5 mph. According to the marine chart, we're over the California Seamount (an underwater mountain). We're surrounded by many kinds of seabirds. A big gull-type bird has made his home on our bowsprit. Ann named him "Sam," the first name of the poet who wrote *The Ancient Mariner*, that classic story about a man and an albatross. Sam perches on the bowsprit for hours at a time, surveying his aquatic kingdom and preening his feathers. I walked to the bow and talked to him. He looks at me in the eye and maintains a haughty silence. I don't frighten him at all. Every few hours he flies off to find food which I'm sure he finds in abundance; this part of the Pacific is teeming with surface fish. *He* has no trouble catching fish. *I* can't catch any.

When the sun is low on the evening horizon, the fish swimming about us seem to turn into luminescent silver, blue, green, and gold missiles. The inboard wells furnish an unequalled marine view, a real aquarium for our private pleasure. When it's still daylight outside, below in the galley (where the two wells are located), darkness is setting in. We peer into these 15-inch square, iron-sided holes through the bottom of the boat and see a perfectly framed moving picture of multi-colored yellowtails swimming lazily underneath. As they pass by, they turn on their sides sometimes, seeming to look up and examine us as we are examining them. Other small four-inch brownish fish without side fins swim into the wells, actually getting in Ann's way when she dips a pan into the well for seawater. She says they're as bold and brazen as Sam. Evidently the birds and fish don't know fear of humans.

Later

We used seawater regularly for bathing and for washing our hair. I still do, and I still shave daily and wash dishes, clothes, etc., with seawater. With a good, soft liquid dish soap, it works quite well. Freshwater at sea is too hard to get to waste it on washing things; it's just for drinking, cooking, and toothbrushing.

June 18

I meditated in the captain's chair on deck for a while at sunset. Sam sat on the tip of the bowsprit arranging his feathers, keeping imperturbable balance in a 25 mph wind. All sails are flying, wind and lumpy seas directly on the beam. Our ship drives on, steering herself, lurching and rolling regularly in slow, deliberate movements. We've been out three weeks and are well into the Pacific.

Here I am, sailing the Pacific Ocean in my own small felucca, heading for the Sandwich Islands! Hard to believe, I think, but absolutely true. I thought of the first time I went to sea. In a 43-foot Liberty ship, going across the Pacific and on to Calcutta, India. The very first night on that ship, I was standing at the bow looking at the sunset as I did tonight. I felt the same then as I feel now, many years later: "I'm off on a great adventure; may it never cease!" Tonight I realized that it hasn't ceased, that it's been one grand adventure after all! My felucca is a grand and beautiful vessel, and it has taken me to Paradise.

Later

The felucca is a good, comfortable sailing vessel. My *Frisco Felucca II* was just an empty hull off a steel lifeboat, lying upside-down on a dock in Alameda when I bought her from the Matson Steamship Company for $150. After towing the boat to Vallejo and cleaning her up, my friend Greg Baker helped me to motor her to Sausalito.

The nameplate on the bow of this galvanized iron lifeboat said:

Built: 1941, Perth Amboy, New Jersey
Length: 35 feet
Beam: 12 feet 6 inches
Depth   [gunwale to bottom]: 5 feet

With the help of Greg and some other friends, we built bulk-heads, installed frames, and covered the deck with tongue-and-groove fir planking. Then we had settees and bunks plus a bricked-in fireplace installed. Covering the entire interior with wall-to-wall red carpet made her quite homey in an elegant way. Ann added many decorative touches and suggested additions such as one bulkhead in solid mirrors. We put up double bunks athwartships (side-to-side instead of fore-and-aft) and the smaller after-cabin bunks could be curtained off. This central room was what we called our "saloon"; it measured 14 x 12 feet and had full headroom.

Then we went up to Healdsburg, my old hometown in Sonoma County, and cut huge fir trees with 15" diameter trunks from my mountain property on the Russian River. We trailered the poles to Sausalito and installed them with the help of friends. We used them for masts, bowsprit, and boomkin. Each installation called for a party where we commanded the help of every friend we could entertain—all was done with good humor, and the friends performed with great good pace.

In order to make the vessel stable and steady in big ocean seas, we poured five tons of wet cement into the bilge bottom area. This weight made her ride easy, like a large ship at sea under sail, even when the weather became frightening. The eucalyptus wooden yards to which the lateen sails were laced (so that the yard could be hoisted up the mast 40 feet into the air) were cut from the hills that surround Sausalito. Only saplings (4" in diameter at the bottom were our choices) were cut.

After Ann had moved out of her "sky room" apartment on the 19th floor of a Nob Hill apartment house and into my vessel in Richardson's Bay, we decided on a name: the *Phantom*. We selected that name because its black hull and ancient-looking rigging made it look quite mysterious and otherworldly. However, after about a month, we made the decision to buck tradition and defy the "bad-luck" theory about changing a boat's name; we changed the name to the *Frisco Felucca II*. That name meant more because of the historic lore concerning the name and its clear reference to earlier sailing vessels in general and, in particular, those that populated San Francisco Bay in such great numbers less than a century earlier and which looked so much like

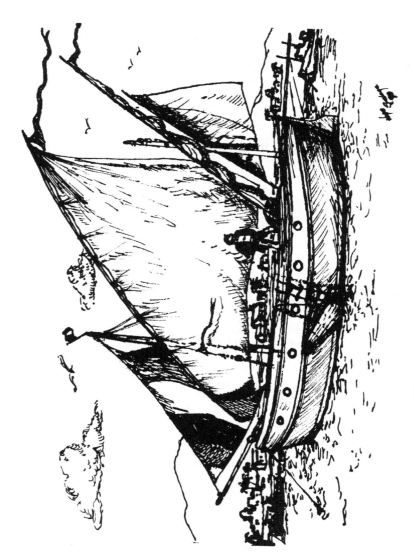

Thus was the Frisco Felucca II *born.*

what we had created. I also had a sailing model of my first felucca on board. Later I had to add the "II" because I realized that my first felucca had to be the *Frisco Felucca I*; and my present 40-foot, two-masted, lateen-rigged vessel is the *Frisco Felucca III*.

Thus was the *Frisco Felucca II* born.

June 19

We were talking about how comfortable this trip has been when a new thought occurred to us. The *Felucca* could easily be dismantled for shipment aboard a freighter. All that would be needed would be to take out several bolts to remove the 15-foot bowsprit and the 10-foot boomkin off the back of the boat; within half an hour the boat will be down to 35 feet long. The masts would have to be taken out with a crane or by several men and could be left on deck with the other pieces. I could make four chocks to support her in an upright position and she would be ready for shipment, say, from Honolulu to San Francisco. It could be carried on a freighter as a "deck load." The ease with which this could be done would make transporting her quite inexpensive. An elaborate cradle, such as one that would be needed for a typical deep-hulled sailing yacht, would not have to be built.

Another advantage of shipping the *Felucca* as a deck load is that we could go aboard her while she's on the freighter. The captains of each vessel could entertain each other on their own boats in the usual manner of marine protocol. We could cut expenses by sleeping (and cooking) aboard the *Felucca*. With these cost-cutting methods, we could afford the expense of shipping her rather easily.

And we discussed hiring passage to India and sailing to the Maldive Islands as Alan Villiers did. I'd like to get a 100-foot "zaruk" (a lateen-rigged Indian dhow) and learn more fine details about handling lateens from the Arabs and the Indians, the people who invented this highly efficient sailing method. I read Villiers' account of his passage on an Arab dhow through the Indian Ocean and am surprised that he didn't mention the extra things that lateen sails will do compared to a Marconi or gaff-rigged, two- or three-masted modern sailing vessel. He wrote, "No watches were kept and there was no semblance of sea style . . . no wheel turns. As for steering, the mates or one of the sailors took the tiller whenever he felt like it . . . ." He said that sailors at the tiller stayed close by it until "it occurred" to someone else to relieve him and that "tricks of five or six hours," maybe even all day, were not uncommon. Villiers didn't realize that lateen rigs will naturally steer themselves.

Lateen-rigged ships will steer themselves on many points of the wind. All of mine, including this *Frisco Felucca II*, have done so. Don't the Indian-Arab dhows self-steer? I suggest that these "tricks of five or six hours" meant that the helmsman was ordered to stay by the wheel but was not in fact steering, but was simply standing by. How much weather helm, if any, do these dhows use? I'll find the answers to these questions and similar ones when I get to India. Yes, India and her dhows are next on my horizon.

Some of the larger flying fish that have landed on deck have four wings. While cleaning one of them, I noticed the insides were almost devoid of entrails and that they have long hollow sections three-quarters their length. Their lightweight bones—as well as their "wings"—are like birds, enough to enable them to fly as far and as high as they do.

The galley stove went out, perhaps for the duration of this voyage. I can't relight it because there is water in the kerosene. It seems to be two-thirds kerosene and one-third water. The fifty gallons I bought in Puerto Vallarta must have been watered for the gringo. Running out of cooking fuel in the middle of the ocean makes for a real problem. I'll have to figure out a way to get the water out of the kerosene.

Later

We'd gotten that kerosene in San Bartolome, Mexico, a few months earlier and, at the time, had no reason to worry about it. Actually, getting into San Bartolome and finding the kerosene had turned into a fine experience. After many days' sailing from Sausalito to Mexico, Ann and I had felt we deserved a few relaxing days, so we took them in Ensenada just before we anchored at San Bartolome. We did some of the things American tourists do in Mexico by walking around and exploring Ensenada and the nearby countryside, but we mostly stayed close to the *Felucca* and relaxed as much as possible. We visited with various other mariners in and around Ensenada's harbor, and they visited us, seemingly charmed by Ann's good graces and the *Felucca's* unusual appearance. By this time, all three of us were seasoned ocean sailors, and I like to think we showed it.

One delightful event we enjoyed at Ensenada was Chuck Rogers' visit. He spent part of his vacation with us. He brought his professional camera from Channel 13 and took extensive footage of us in town and out sailing the *Felucca* around the harbor. The footage he shot then was combined with the earlier films taken in San Francisco Bay and was shown on Channel 13 in January as a news documentary. A friend of Chuck's, a newspaper reporter, came with him from San Diego and wrote a feature article for two newspapers about our unusual vessel and the cruise. We thoroughly enjoyed their visit, our parties with many other mariners on our various types of boats, the people of Ensenada, and our change of pace, but soon enough it was time to move on. We'd become convinced about the seaworthiness of our boat, and we were eager to resume Our Trip down the coast of Mexico.

So we chose a sunny, clear morning with favorable winds and tide, and hoisted anchor from Ensenada's harbor. I had asked four skippers who were heading south to give us a tow around Punta Banda, fifteen miles across the bay from Ensenada, but none could oblige us. I had not trusted such a light breeze and found good reason for that mistrust after we had sailed out about five miles into Todos Santos Bay. The wind dropped to nothing in the space of a few minutes and left us totally becalmed. But by this time, we weren't bothered or worried.

We had no schedule anymore. Why should we be upset because we were not rushing along under full sail? We were both healthy, well-fed, and happy to be with each other. During a calm, we had learned that we could wash (ourselves, our clothes, our boat), we could read, we could write, we could sunbathe—we could relax and rest, in other words. Sailing can be restful and relaxing, of course, but a change is as good as a rest and we came to cherish the changes that the calmed winds and water offered us. So we sat, a few days after Christmas, still and quiet in the middle of a Mexican bay in the *Felucca II* with idle sails and played gin rummy.

A slight breeze blew in early the second day of our departure from Ensenada, so we set our attention on getting around Punta Banda, a small island not far from Ensenada. The prevailing wind there in Todos Santos Bay was from the west. One must sail west to get out of the Bay, and we learned how difficult that is without an engine. Except for the usual early morning easterlies, adverse breezes were the rule; we faced those breezes for a full forty-eight hours only to find that we were only ten miles away from Ensenada. When I made that calculation and announced our location to Ann, she simply smiled and shrugged her shoulders. So what? she seemed to say. *We had no schedule.* There are no schedules in Paradise that can't be changed without thinking twice. What are forty-eight hours in one lifetime when you have what we had?

We sailed away easily and out of the bay, heading south down the coast, with no difficulties whatsoever in the following morning's brisk, favorable wind. We were amazed to see so many fish! At that time of year, it is common in those waters for the sea to have a "red tide." This is a reddish sea caused by a surge in the volume of sea plankton. This "red tide" draws hundreds of fish to feed on the bounty. Porpoises and whales enjoy the feast, too, and it was a special delight to watch these huge animals. The whales gamboled about like children at play, plunging under our boat on one side and leaping from the water on the other side, spouting profusely as they soared into the air. It seemed as if there were scores of giant whales and hundreds of glistening porpoises playing "follow-the-leader." They seemed to function in small groups, and each group seemed to be going somewhere in particular, somewhere in a different direction from the others. These animals and fish were obviously enjoying their feast. It was also a satisfying and fascinating sight to see.

In retrospect, I've come to understand that sailing down the Baja California coast with no chart besides a Mexican-language AAA road map is not something I'd advise someone else to do. It seemed reasonable at the time, and we did it. We'd sailed this far from San Francisco, I thought, and we'd get further. And it was fun to watch the reactions of more experienced sailors to find out we had no engine, no charts, no chronometer, and only a hand compass and a cheap plastic sextant. The weather was predictably pleasant in general, and we could sail in closer to the shore when we needed to compare the land with what we could not make out on the road map.

After eight days of sailing down the coast in light, variable winds, our passenger had to leave us. We didn't see any port on shore and the road map indicated none anywhere near us, so we flagged down the first vessel we saw. It was a large fishing boat, and it was headed straight for us. By this time, we were used to other boats coming up close to us. Many went out of their way, often actually changing course to come alongside and hail us. They were intrigued by our lateen-rigged vessel. Some would shout, "Is that a dhow?" Some would imitate Chinese (badly) and shout, "Is that boat a junk?" Most would just ask simply, "What kind of boat is that?" A few skippers assumed we were in trouble and had had to rig some makeshift sail; they'd ask if we needed help.

That's what this skipper did. He came right alongside and asked worriedly if we needed assistance. I told him that I had a passenger aboard who needed to get to the nearest port and asked him if he could take my passenger. The captain paused a moment, then asked, "Do you know where you are?"

I tried to match his melodramatic manner with my "No!" reply.

He responded with what I am sure was an internal slap on his knee. "Look over there. That's Cedros Island."

Cedros Island is one of the biggest peaks in the Baja waterline. At this particular moment, navigating by road map seemed a quite foolish thing to be doing, and I suddenly felt about an inch tall and quite embarrassed. So I waved to the skipper of the fishing boat and turned the *Felucca* towards Cedros Island.

Two days later, we sailed happily around Kelp Point into Turtle Bay with a 15 mph wind behind us, our fair weather jib, lateen main and mizzen all drawing smartly. As the small village of San Bartolome came into view, we saw five yachts anchored in the harbor. There was also a tour boat that looked as if it held twenty-five to thirty passengers. As we were looking about for a favorable anchorage site just a little further in, the wind suddenly stopped completely and we were becalmed again. We only had about a half-mile or so to what appeared to be a fine anchorage, so I pulled the skiff around and attached about thirty feet of line to her from the *Felucca's* bow. Skippers, crew, and passengers of power boats, sailing yachts, tour boats, and fishing boats carefully watched every thrust of my oars as I towed the *Felucca* the last few hundred yards to anchor. They were intensely curious about this strange-looking boat that obviously didn't have a working engine. Under hundreds of watchful eyes, we dropped anchor about a hundred yards from the dock. Before we took our passenger ashore, we went below for refreshments and to bid him goodbye. We took him ashore and waved farewell.

I'd previously read in *Sea* magazine about San Bartolome and Turtle Bay's anchorages and facilities. The magazine had mentioned a large-girthed man named "Gordo" as the man to see about purchasing fuel, repairing engines, and tending to other motor-related mechanical concerns. We reasoned—correctly, as things developed—that he would be the person from whom we could buy some kerosene for our lamps and stove. We started our search for Gordo and were sidetracked by a store that had supplies to replenish our larder. We got what we needed and tried to buy some tequila and beer. To my surprise and dismay, we discovered that alcohol sale is illegal in Baja California! The store clerk noticed my reaction to this Mexican reality and quietly arranged for me to buy a smidgen of tequila (for a ridiculously high price!). We loaded up on drinking water, too, paying dearly for it. Lower California is so dry that the supply of freshwater is a constant problem and an expensive one to solve. We returned replenished to the *Felucca* to spend the night, sipping a preciously small amount of expensive but genuinely Mexican tequila before we went to bed.

The next morning we returned to shore and resumed our search for Gordo. Ann spotted him first. "Look. At the end of the dock. There's a fat man. Maybe that's Gordo."

As we drew nearer, we could see that the man was well on his way to full and complete intoxication. He was idly conversing with a young fellow while trying to lean on a fifty-gallon drum. He kept losing his balance while standing and would fall/reach for the drum to retain his stance, but then he would let it go and start to fall again. He wasn't fat, though; his size was caused by an abundance of huge muscles, so heavily laid in the upper torso he looked like a professional wrestler. He had coal black hair and dark, limpid eyes, full of observant expression even while drunk. His two upper front teeth were missing.

I said, "Are you Gordo? I'd like to buy some kerosene."

91

He answered, *"Mbxsa akjkjeda podia,"* or something that sounded like that.

I said, "How much is a gallon of kerosene?"

He said, "I'm Gordo. Petroleo, petroleo," and started drawing numbers in the dust on the drum with his right index finger.

After two or three minutes of this, we had gotten nowhere. So I said, "We have to go now. We'll come back later and buy some petroleum." We started to leave.

Suddenly, Gordo stood fully erect and asked us in perfect, although accented, English, "Which boat is yours?"

I pointed to the black *Felucca* not far from the end of the dock where we were standing.

"Negro barco?" Gordo asked. His eyes lit up with a broad smile showing a gap from the missing two front teeth, and he rushed towards me with his huge arms outstretched, and wrapped them around me in a Spanish *brazo* (a welcoming hug). I was afraid for a moment that he was going to kiss me. I exchanged the *brazo* with him and patted him on his back while he pounded mercilessly on mine. Ann stood by in astonishment.

"Come wit' me," Gordo commanded. He grabbed one of my arms and one of Ann's and pulled. "I'll get you anything you want, but first you must come to my house!"

In Spanish and English he made complimentary statements about Ann, about me, about our parents, and—mainly—about the *Felucca* and about my rowing her to her anchorage. He had been one of the many onlookers when I did that, and he was quite favorably impressed. He was very pleased that someone would do that because that's how it's "always" been done, he said.

We walked, or rather he took us, about two hundred yards down the beach to his home. Almost all of the houses in San Bartolome were like Gordo's: small clapboard structures that look as if they were built by anyone but a carpenter and then painted by children in beautiful Easter egg pastel colors. That method of construction suits the climate there, and the color is a delicate balance to the sunbaked earth and the brilliant colors of the sunbaked, desert-like countryside.

Gordo was handily successful in conversing with us in his combination of English and Spanish and our almost total lack of Spanish. We discovered that he had twenty-six children and grandchildren and that he continues the possibilities of having

92

more children by cavorting with several girlfriends. When Ann teased him about having so many girlfriends, Gordo flopped his huge fist over his heart and bellowed out, "I gotta love!"

His (second) wife stood at the stove as we talked, cooking turtle stew. She's a slight, attractive woman in her late twenties and was shyly smiling constantly. Yes, she was six months pregnant. Gordo introduced us to her and to several children who varied in age from one to six. He commanded us to sit down at a small oilcloth-covered table and commanded his wife to "Get da beer." She brought two warm six-packs that Gordo opened quickly and effortlessly. He proposed a toast to Ann and me, another to *Felucca*, and a third to the world in general. He was getting more and more intoxicated. His third command was to his wife to get us our lunch. She served all of us: the children, her husband, Ann, me, and Gordo's young companion who'd accompanied us from the dock. All but Mrs. Gordo enjoyed an exquisitely delicious turtle stew; she spent the entire time serving us and obeying Gordo's commands.

From the kitchen window we could see all the harbor and the boats in it. Gordo kept praising the looks of our boat. Because of her high freeboard, tilted bowsprit, lateen rig and flying pennants, along with her flat black hull and yellow boot topping, the *Felucca* stood out like a ship from the distant past. The *Felucca* was a hit with Gordo. We made a date for Gordo to join us aboard ship for dinner, thanked him and his wife profusely for the wonderful meal and hospitality, and returned to the *Felucca*.

Gordo didn't show up for dinner. We had thought he might not, considering the amount of alcohol he had consumed. The following morning, we went shopping to try to find something nice for these hospitable people, and we decided upon the four pairs of new children's tennis shoes that someone had given us to give away. We took them over to Gordo's, but Mrs. Gordo said she didn't know where to find him. She also told us that, yes, he was "muy borracho" (very drunk) the night before and collapsed asleep at home. She patted the baby in her stomach with both hands and said to me, "If baby I have boy, I name 'Tomaso' for you," and to Ann she said, "If girl, I name 'Anita' for you."

So, in a very roundabout way, we got our kerosene—the kerosene with the water in it.

June 20

Sam the seabird gave us a surprise yesterday. He turned out to be a she. Sam mated last night and the gender of both birds was obvious. They were both oblivious to our interested stares. Both Sam and her new boyfriend have brown and white wings, but as is often the case in the avian world, the male has the more colorful markings. Sam—the female, remember—has a gray head and breast with white feet, and that's about it. Her boyfriend has a pure white head and breast with bright red feet. Then this morning, we saw two turtles mating. They were attached together, both upside-down, one underneath the other with strange grins on their faces. The boat passed within fifty feet of them and they didn't move. They didn't seem to notice us but just floated lazily on the water, obviously enjoying "doing their thing."

Good grief! It must be the mating season out here.

June 22

It's the first day of summer; the weather is warm and sunny, the sea is a wonderously translucent blue, and today we entered the trade winds at last! It's a day for celebration. The wind has backed around and is coming from slightly abaft the beam. I changed the sails into the "Cross of St. James" for downwind running. Even in light air today, the boat sails well. Tonight we opened our last bottle of wine and enjoyed Ann's delicious spaghetti and meatballs for dinner on deck. As we ate, an enormous turtle at least four feet across floated past with flippers leisurely and slowly balancing himself so that he could watch us. Maybe he looked at us and thought us to be a giant turtle. I wonder what turtles eat?

Ann and I took baths in seawater tonight on the foredeck in our old-fashioned galvanized tub with a big plastic bucket (with rope attached), a scrub brush, washcloth, and liquid dish detergent. Our hair becomes very soft and squeaky clean feeling when washed in seawater. After bathing we took turns sluicing each other with buckets of ocean water. It was quite refreshing. Ann, her lovely body stretched out with her head propped on a soft green pillow, remarked, "This is the best vacation I've ever had." I

94

told her that my dreams were coming true because of her. Without Ann's emotional, psychological, physical, and intellectual help, I certainly would not have been able to make my dream the wonderful reality it had become. Tonight was not the only night when I was highly conscious of Ann's importance to me, but tonight it was especially meaningful.

June 23—2,000 miles from Hawaii, the 26th day, drifting south

The *Felucca* continues to steer herself, wheel lashed. As we're not in a shipping lane, we've been getting eight or more hours' sleep every night while the *Felucca* takes care of her own steering. We've been in a calm at least sixty-five percent of the twenty-six days since we left Mexico. These twenty-six days seemed like a week at the most.

That's a good thing, I think, because this voyage has turned into one that's lasting a lot longer than I'd expected. I'd thought we'd be in Hilo after six weeks at the very most. We've been at sea now for almost four weeks, and we're still over 2,000 miles from Hawaii. Now that the trade winds have kicked in, though, we ought to make up for lost time and get there relatively soon. We need to, as we brought food for only about six weeks.

Later

My using the lateen rigging has taught me a great deal about sailing and about the many advantages that kind of rigging has over the more ordinary types of rigging. In the Mediterranean and on the Portuguese and Spanish coasts where Arab influence persists today, lateen-rigged craft with from one to four masts and known generically as the "caravel" (or *caravela latina*) remained the principal coastal vessels for centuries. Columbus used such craft for his explorations. By 1890, it was the most popularly used vessel in San Francisco Bay, and lateen-rigged vessels plied the Bay and related environs up and down the West Coast.

On a lateen rig, the great length and size of the yard antenna to which the sail is lashed aloft limits the size of the ship unless additional masts are added. The yard on the *Frisco Felucca II* was 48 feet; Columbus' caravel, the *Nina*, was said to be a three-masted lateen-rigged 70-foot vessel whose yard antenna was approximately 60 feet. Even today in the Persian Gulf, one can see three-masted caravel types (dhows) still carrying cargo and, quite often, engaging in smuggling and pirating activities.

I recently spent almost a year and a half along the Persian Gulf from Baghdad to Portuguese Goa in southern India. I saw several shipyards that still repair old sailing ships and build new ones in the old style which to them is quite traditional (however, they only build the smaller ones today). They use the same type of tools and equipment that were used to build Columbus' *Nina*, and they tend to rely on all handwork with no electricity or other power devices.

The *caravela latina*, with its ability to sail close into the wind and to beat upwind (compared to what a square rig can do) was recognized as the most able windward-maneuvering sailing vessel of its time, one that was well suited for exploring new waters or pirating in old ones. In the Maritime Museum in Paris opposite the Eiffel Tower is a 12-foot sailing model of a three-masted caravel of a type called the *xebec*. It was this type of lateen-rigged vessel that Henry the Navigator's sailing captain, Bartolomeu Dias, took around Africa's Cape of Good Hope in the early 1400s. He went the hard way, from east to west. Upwind! Lateen-rigged caravels have played a major role in exploration voyages for centuries.

Nowadays, many conventional sailors ridicule the lateen rig because they imagine it to be necessary to move the yard from one side of the mast to the other with each change of direction. I can say flatly that this is not true. My own experience with lateen rigs as well as my extensive observation and research with others confirms as fact the lack of need to change the yard. I have seen, for example, three-masted, 90-foot, lateen-rigged dhows maneuvering into Bombay, India, tacking back and forth upwind across the bay without ever moving the yard from one side of the mast to the other. The sails were simply allowed to lie against the smooth mast on one tack and then flow free on the opposite tack. Not once did I see any special complication. Upon turning the vessel to the opposite tack, the jib sheets simply had to be secured to the opposite side of the dhow, but the sheets (or ropes) from the clew (or corner) of the lateeners stayed put. The yards swung

96

easily over against the mast, taking the wind on the opposite side of the sail. There was no raising or lowering or switching.

The same procedure worked everytime with my two-masted *Felucca*. When I came around to the opposite tack, the sails flopped over by themselves; all the single-handed sailor needed to do was secure the jib sheet (rope) on the opposite side. The two lateen sails needed no tending in order to complete the maneuver single-handedly with all moves handled from the aft cockpit area. If I were on a long tack, like this crossing from Mexico to Hawaii, where the wind was almost always from the same side, I could then change the yard to the opposite side in order to avoid chaffing the sail against the mast. Chaff was minimal, but over a many-day period it would justify changing the yard to the opposite side.

It's not that hard a trick to bring the vessel up straight into the wind until the sail is loose and luffing. Then, all that's needed is to grab the bottom of the yard and pull it to the other side of the mast; the top of the yard will follow and the boat is on the other tack. The yard and sail fall in on the opposite side of the mast and, *voila!* No chaff!

In all the time I sailed the *Frisco Felucca II*, however, I never changed the yard to the other side except once; on this 3,500 mile trip from Puerto Vallarta, Mexico, to Hilo, Hawaii. And one night as I was coming south from Cabo San Lucas to Puerta Vallarta, I asked Ann to take the wheel and twice circle the *Felucca* about single-handed, just to practice.

"Suppose I fell over the side," I said, "and you needed to go back and pick me up?"

The first thing to do in a man-overboard drill is to throw a life jacket or ring overboard instantly. Then the boat needs to circle back to the "man overboard." Ann took the wheel and wore the vessel about in three concentric circles as we sailed slowly south under a magnificent moon to Puerto Vallarta, another portion of Paradise. I remained at the bow to observe the first coming about and then went below to start coffee. Ann easily handled the entire rest of the drill alone because steering was all that was needed except to move the jib line across to the opposite side on each tack. In heavy air, more caution must be taken. But because the lateen sail has no massive boom on its bottom edge (the sail's "foot"), it is a much safer rig mechanically and quite easy "to come about." A heavy boom on a ten-ton sailer can wreak havoc as it races across the vessel, sweeping everything before it. In a lateen-rigged vessel there is only the loose-footed cloth sail that sweeps across. If the boom hits you, it can do serious damage; if the lateen sail's foot hits you, it's no worry. And if you have the additional sail already made up and stowed before you leave port, you can rerig your caravel to become a "ship rig" by simply taking down the main lateens and rerigging the masts with square sails. All this rerigging can be down with relative ease at sea. I marvel at how few sailors know of the many advantages of lateen rigging.

June 25—Latitude 13:30, too far south, bypass Hawaii

A fresh breeze blew all night between 20 and 25 mph. We sailed with the wind on or slightly forward of the beam almost in the trough of the whitecapped sea. We have been down to 13:30 latitude and must start heading north to latitude 20—360 miles north—if we expect to get to Hawaii. If we don't get that correct latitude, we'll bypass Hawaii completely. We made 88 miles of westing and 11 miles northing in the last twenty-four hours. I can hardly wait to calculate the mileage after the wind has been abaft for a few days. The *Felucca* continues to steer herself.

Yesterday I mounted the tri-color jib behind the bigger second jib on the bowsprit. The boat seems to sail better with additional canvas forward. This is my working canvas in a beam wind. When the breeze shifts permanently to the northeast, I'll be able to put up my last big sail, a square sail 9 feet long by 4 feet deep; that should give us additional mileage downwind. This small sail is carried under the bowsprit and is called a *spritsail*, or *water sail*. The only thing that seriously concerns me is that the mainsail will rip and tear in a fresh breeze. I have materials to replace this sail in the event that I mistakenly leave it up too long in too strong a wind. We'll see.

Today Ann beat me at gin rummy. But I won at chess. We play chess on a 17-inch cowhide leather chessboard with five-inch wood and bone men that keep steady even in this 25 mph beam wind. The chessboard was given to me by my Sausalito friend and fellow boat-dweller, Ale Eckstrom. I remember his leather clothes and red hair-in-a-braid-with-a-brass-ring-at-the-end (like an 18th century sailor) each time Ann and I play chess.

Sometimes, like last night, while Ann is sleeping, I get up in the night and go on deck behind the small wheelhouse and sit in my captain's chair. It's especially comfortable because I've cut off most of its leg lengths, making it sit very low. I feel at home within this circle, more at home here than at a dock, in a berth, or in some crowded anchorage. The *Frisco Felucca II* is my home. Our front and backyards are the seas. When the ocean gets rough and white, we either turn and go with the wind or hove to into it. We don't fight the sea or the wind; we agree with them and share affectionately with them. They're all part of our home on the sea.

Later

The unique little town of Sausalito will always be my home port. It played a major role in leading me to become a fan of lateen rigging, it was where I got both my *Felucca I* and *Felucca II*, and the many wonderful people in and around its waters; each had their place in helping me realize my dreams. When I first arrived in Sausalito, I knew I'd "come home." I'd already circled the world twice—once as a merchant seaman and once as a private traveller—and I thought I'd seen it all. But Sausalito had a peculiar, special feeling for me. My experience is that it's true that there are good people to be found all over the world, but I truly believe they tend to congregate in and around Sausalito.

The port is a veritable captain's paradise with seagoing boats calling weekly from around the world. The town tumbles down the side of a mountain into San Francisco Bay, and the place gave birth (berth?) to what has become a thriving artist's community and houseboat colony. Half-built boats, boats converted into floating houses, and things that can only be called "floating works of art" with people living in them are anchored out off Sausalito in Richardson's Bay. Older maps call it "Carmalita Bay," and the Indians call(ed) it "Rainbow Bay." During the rainy season, there are sometimes as many as three or four complete rainbows, and both their ends are often visible. It's a special sight to see someone's house or boat on the water brilliantly colored by a rainbow's base. Abandoned boats and parts of boats can still be found around the area to offer great opportunities for the energetic, enterprising do-it-yourselfers. For over forty years after I first arrived in that enchanted little place, I've always come back. It's been my home since I first saw it in 1948.

Jean "Yanko" Varda

That was the year I was attending the University of California at Berkeley. P.T. Stanton, a great brass cornet player and his traditional jazz band were playing at a waterfront tavern called "The Gladhand"; it stood on wooden pilings over the water. The view over the Bay was fantastic. People in the tavern and outside on its deck could see Raccoon Straits, Angel Island, Alcatraz Island, and the greatest seaside city in the world, San Francisco. I graduated from UCB and eventually found my way to Sausalito, where I settled in a small house on Main Street, near Sally Stanford's famous Valhalla Restaurant; she was a loveable old madam (retired, I thought at the time) who became Mayor of Sausalito.

Shortly after I got to Sausalito, I met Jean Varda ("Yanko" to his many friends). He was a colorful artist in his late sixties and he served many functions—among these functions was "guru" to long-haired artists of all kinds. They flocked to him, paying court

100

to him aboard his side-wheeler ferryboat *Vallejo* that was his home. He was a great storyteller, an entertaining and talented artist, and he had snow white hair that hung down from his bald, tanned and usually bare head to his collar. His costume regularly included sandals or tennis shoes, baggy dark grey flannel slacks, and a bulky sweater regardless of the weather. His dark Greek eyes would flash with anger and then sparkle with mirth and gaiety. He was exuberantly honest, and I was always pleased when Varda would stop briefly and talk with me when we chanced to meet. The subject of our talks always got around to lateen-rigged sailing vessels. When we went to his ferryboat, the *Vallejo*, to continue our interesting talks, he would sit at his main table and usually sip wine while he did pencil drawings for me to illustrate his explanation of the wonders of the lateen rig.

Yanko hosted so many artistic and wonderful people, and he treated us all with his special care that made each one of us feel as if we were his favorite person. Some of his more famous guests included Henry Miller, Anaïs Nin, Salvadore Dali, and many others, and I learned from his stories and from other people that his early days in Paris saw him happily engaged with people like Picasso, Nijinsky, Duchamp, Braque, and others. Someone had written elsewhere something about how it wasn't the famous people who visited Varda and then made Sausalito exciting nearly so much as it was Varda himself, as it was his light and his energy that fused together all those poets and painters and sculptors and potters and sailors and singers and actors to make magic happen on the Sausalito waterfront and in her harbor.

I suppose I was one of Varda's flock. He was well-known as an outstanding sailor, and fun-loving people of all ages were delighted to fill his 22-foot galvanized iron lifeboat that he'd converted to a sound sailing vessel for his regular Sunday outings on the Bay. Those outings were legendary, and it was an awe-inspiring sight to see them under full lateen-rigged sail. The sails were painted in Varda's designs—they reminded most of us of Picasso's work but we liked Yanko's better—the hull was painted with huge, expressive eyes on the bow with flowing flames of bold green, orange, and black streaming back to the stern from the bow. With such extravagant color, such wild patterns, and such wonderful energy from the crowds of wine-drinking, pot-smoking revelers on board, Varda's Sunday afternoon boat would have been impressive enough with ordinary rigging, but it was his lateen rigging that confirmed the very special style of the man, his boat, and his undertakings.

Varda was a feisty old man, and when his sailboat began to get beyond where it could be repaired, he got another one, ten feet longer at thirty-two feet. He put three masts on this one and rigged each mast differently: he rigged his signature lateen sail on the foremast, a Chinese sail on the main (middle mast), and a gaff-rigged sail on the after mast—each brilliantly painted in the designs and color that had helped make him famous. In his Greek accent, he called it "mya interrrrrrrrrnational sailin' baht."

The larger boat let him increase the number of guests on his Sunday afternoon sailing parties to sixteen or so beautiful people who sailed with him in great merriment and good high style to Angel Island, about the Bay, through the Gate—wherever the spirits and God's good winds moved him. That man was instrumental in creating an entire era, an age peopled with artists and artistic people with great zest for life and filled with individual, unique boats to live in and to carry them about here on San Francisco Bay and points wherever. His brightly painted lateen-rigged *Chimera* and *Perfida* were brilliant testimonies to his love of life and people, and he inspired many others to create their own marvelous vessels. One written description about him says that he converted these old lifeboats "by his great grace and the enthusiasm of his friends and pupils." It was also said that his two boats (plus others he had over the years) inspired other people to create "peacocks and gold pheasants sailing among seas of albino turkeys on almost every weekend."

When he died (during a trip to Mexico, 1971), his ashes were returned to Sausalito and were scattered by friends into the water under the Golden Gate Bridge, thrown from his felucca into the Pacific's ebbing tide. Sausalito and the rest of the world lost a wonderful man and a great artist when Yanko Varda died.

It was Varda, more than anyone else in Sausalito, who inspired me with his lateen-rigged lifeboats. I wanted a lateen-rigged type of vessel because of how his worked for him as an outstandingly effective sailing vessel. Not long after I met Varda I found a man in Bolinas who was building a 20-foot sailing vessel that he had styled after what he had called a "Frisco Felucca." His project stalled when his money ran out, and I bought his boat and paid him to finish it for me. I called it my *Felucca* and, after many months of happy use, got another one named the *Felucca II*, thereby making that first one the *Felucca I* by default.

That first vessel, the *Felucca*, was and still is a superb sailing vessel, and it was the beginning of my education about the marvels of lateen rigging. For several years after I sold her, this ship of mine sailed with her lateen rig as a commercial fishing boat out of Sausalito. Her new owners, two local boatbuilders and "seat-of-the-pants sailors" Sam Anderson and Steve Webber, reported frequently on her fine performance even 30 miles offshore in a fresh blow. At the time, I had no hint that someday I would take the *Felucca II* on one of the most incredible voyages of my life; that was yet to come, and I was content to sail my *Felucca* in and around Sausalito and the Delta. I guess Sausalito is my "home base" and the *Felucca* on the seas is my only home.

June 27—Starting north, no food, water

I'm still learning about sailing a lateen rig, learning for instance that the rudder should be used only when changing course. If possible, the rudder should not be used at all merely to hold the boat on course; balance the sails and the boat will steer herself. A conventional weather helm—holding the wheel a few spokes opposite the wind to get the most speed—isn't the choice with the *Felucca*. When I've changed the course either upwind or downwind, I ease off the rudder and simultaneously use the mizzen sail or leeboards to influence the steering. In other words, I use little or no "weather helm" on the rudder while the *Felucca* is self-steering.

Ann made an unusual, interesting dinner tonight of jerky and black beans. She cut the meat into small pieces, fried it in bacon fat and then cooked it in her Italian mushroom sauce with garlic and herbs an hour and a half in the pressure cooker. Then she served it over specially seasoned mashed beans. How she manages to make such plebeian fare taste so exquisitely delicious is beyond me.

She made a more unusual, interesting announcement after dinner. She told me that we had just eaten the absolute last of our food. This was a shock, to put it mildly. I had not even the slightest hint that we were even *low* on food supplies, let alone completely out! I demanded to know why she waited to tell me and she explained that she knew there was nothing I could do to get more food out here. After all, she said, there was no supermarket out here and she didn't want me to worry over something I could do nothing about. Now what will we do? I thought we had food to last for another week at least but now we're completely out!

Later—1,000 miles from Hawaii, frenzy fishing

I remember that Ann's announcement upset me terribly. I had gotten us into some difficulties on this voyage with my attitude, but this one was one of the more serious ones. Well, there we sat. Fifty days out from Puerto Vallarta, somewhere between 700 and 1,200 miles from Hawaii, give or take, and no food. No engine. No radio. No wind. Besides the boat, we still had only that $15 Mark IV plastic sextant, one sea chart, a Bulova wristwatch for our chronometer, our Mexican AAA road map, and a pocket compass. For good measure, we had my AAA road map of Honolulu. But we weren't even riding swells. We were sitting dead in the water. Not hungry right this moment, not after such a wonderful meal. But now that meal seemed like a prisoner's last meal before his execution. We were sure to know what hunger really could mean.

That next morning, we both confirmed how right Ann was about being out of food; the only things left to eat were a goodly supply of garlic cloves, some butter, a small bottle of lemon juice and a reasonably well-stocked spice and herb cabinet. Our food supply—or lack of it—was dangerous. We had water for several more days, but we were seriously discussing how we might cook our shoes. I didn't know what to do. Ann seemed much less worried than I. She gently pointed out how many fish were out there and how we could eat fish.

Fish? I hated fishing. Ann knew how I hated fishing! All my life I'd avoided fishing as avidly as possible. Even on this voyage I'd not seriously tried to fish, even though I'd had a line out almost every other day! A friend who knew this about me had tried to help before we left Sausalito. He'd given me four lures with wire leaders, proper lead weights, hooks, some line, and I don't know what else, and he had tried very hard to tell me how to use all this to catch fish. I was desperately wishing I'd paid more attention to his instructions as I sat there in the middle of the Pacific Ocean, watching fish swim and fly all around me, hating even the *idea* of fishing, realizing that I'd probably have to catch some fish or else starve to death . . . . Over the years, I've tried several times to catch fish but at no time did my efforts produce success or pleasure. Indeed, I'd most often been frustrated, thwarted, and otherwise angered when I'd tried to fish. Indeed again, I'd seriously tried fishing just recently, right after we left Puerto Vallarta, trolling and line fishing my heart out, but all was for nought then, too. Each time a fish hit the hook, it would either bite the line and break its way free, or else it would give such a tremendous tug that my fifty-pound test line would snap. Or, most often, I'd just watch the fish watch my lure, snub it, and move away. Once again I had found myself thinking, for the umpteenth time, that I couldn't fish, that I didn't want to fish, and that I *hated* fishing. I tried to decide not to fish, but I kept thinking of things that seemed to make the need for fishing even more urgent. An urgent thing like *starvation*.

I recalled several stories that I'd heard about how other unfortunate mariners had starved to death even as they watched fish break the surface near their boats. Even with the *best* of equipment it's hard to fish at sea, even when one is desperate!

We could eat birds. Seabirds were everywhere. And there was Sam and her boyfriend. That made two large delicious-looking fat ones just waiting for Ann's stew pot. They were certainly in excellent shape: when a cloud of flying fish broke the surface to flee from attacks from the larger fish beneath them, our two birds chased them and overtook and gobbled them down in midair without missing a beat of their strong-winged flight. But how could I *catch* either of them? Those suckers were alert, strong, and Sam was downright *fierce*! Surely her boyfriend was fiercer. If I had a gun, perhaps I could shoot them. Or a net? No net. But even if I caught them, could we eat them? Sam had practically become our pet, somehow always showing up at the end of whatever weather kept her away, always somehow appearing happy to be "home." How could we eat Sam? Or her boyfriend? No, we would not be eating birds.

What about turtles? Almost at the very moment that I'd decided against trying to capture a bird, I saw a giant sea turtle floating nearby; I hoped against hope that he'd just died and was waiting for me to figure out how to haul him aboard. No such luck—he was very much alive as he slowly turned his head towards the *Felucca* and lazily moved his front fins to swim slowly below the surface and out of sight. It looked like he flipped me off with his tail. This desperate sailor would *never* be able to catch a live turtle.

Okay, turtles and birds were out. Well, maybe we could make do by eating the occasional flying fish that floundered on the deck. The last one had fallen aboard five or six days ago, so it was about time for another one. We'd eaten two of them and found them delicious. But we needed food now, not at some unknown future date when a flying fish might or might not miscalculate and bang into our sails by accident. Eating flying fish would be totally undependable as a solution for our hunger. I couldn't think of anything else except somehow learning how to fish.

All I had to do to see countless fish was look over the side. A long, graceful ripple was being created by what appeared to be a huge silver fish at least six feet long, lazily undulating its way past us right beneath the surface. Shadows near it and elsewhere all around us made it clear that there was an abundance of fish. I knew that various types of fish are plentiful in the Pacific near the 20th parallel where we were: shark, swordfish, sailfish, porpoise, Orcas, whale, Dorado and more—including the ubiquitous flying fish. I'd seen the Dorado frequently, even at that moment, and knew them to be blunt-nosed, iridescent blue-green and silver fish with brilliant yellow tails. They average two to three feet in length and are also called Sailors' Dolphin, Yellowtail, or Mahi-Mahi, and are of the percoid family. I knew that at least some of those shadows in the water must have been Dorado. Fish everywhere, and I knew I had to catch at least one. And soon.

So with a sigh I headed below to locate the forgotten fishing gear. I made several stops along the way, trying to find any reason to justify not fishing. Perhaps I might even discover some food aboard that wasn't there earlier. In this frame of mind, I idly picked up the log and turned to a page at random. I read:

June 21: fish are as abundant as I've even seen. Their pecking order is on display daily. Big ones eat little ones. Like humans.

The Orcas, a shark which resembles a porpoise, feeds on Dorado. Enthralling: a fierce nine-foot Orca took a quick-moving three-foot Dorado by the middle of its back, held it midair in his mouth like a knife in a pirate's teeth and dove into the depths with its dinner. Last evening we marveled at shoals of flying fish, Dorado in chase swimming at the same rapid speed a seagull flies. The winged flying fish seemed to be in magnificent panic, soaring up to about a *hundred feet* in altitude and spanning what looked like a distance equivalent to the length of a football field before they splashed back into the water! The Dorado fish leapt out of the sea and practically walked on the water, leaving a boiling wake behind them and using their tails for balance, and snatched the slowest flying fish in midair. The Dorado were making a strange "Br-r-r-r-r" noise when they started their skittish walk across the water, making me think they were making "Hmmmmhmmmm, good" noises before they had their feast! And if it wasn't bad enough for the flying fish to have the Dorado after them from below, there were many clouds of seabirds, including our two "pets," after them from in the air from above.

Everybody was eating fish but us! Even reading the log was pointing me inexorably towards taking fishing gear in hand and landing a fish or two for dinner! So I stowed the log and finally pulled out what fishing equipment I had left. It wasn't much. There were several tri-hooks and one single hook, one lure, and a few short lengths of line. I guess I'd lost the rest in the last abortive fishing attempt back near Puerto Vallarta.

This time, I didn't even try to troll. It didn't work before, I thought, and I didn't see any way I could make it work this time. So I simply tossed the lure over the side. The line was short enough so that I could watch the lure and also watch the reactions of fish as they considered it. We had entered an area where the water was crystal clear, and I could now see the fish as if they were suspended in midair below the boat. The boat was sailing slowly in light air, and the fish seemed to enjoy swimming in the shadow underneath us. I watched scores of iridescent fish as they played alongside and below the *Felucca* and as they rapidly swam over to my lure, sniffed at it, and darted away. Several Dorado investigated the lure. Each one was quick to get near it but almost as quick to disregard it, treating it as if it were just a piece of driftwood being towed along by a big boat.

107

In anger, I yanked the lure away from a big Dorado as he snubbed my lure. To my surprise, several Dorado, including the big one, were suddenly very interested. They chased the lure. I stopped yanking it and they stopped pursuing it. I yanked it and they followed. So I yanked it out of the water. They followed somewhat, some even poking their noses out of the water to watch where that lure was going. I experimented: by trolling the lure, the fish treated it like a yellow fish, almost ignoring it. By yanking it around underwater, I found that the fish got interested. By pulling it out of the water, I thought they were ready to strike. So I decided to make my lure act like a flying fish.

I tied the lure to about fifteen feet of ¼-inch Mexican rope and tied it to the end of my seven-foot gaffer's rod. Then I skimmed the lure back and forth on the top of the water, trying not to let it stop or sink. Then the Dorado became visibly more agitated and excited and began swimming rapidly in circles around the lure as it moved just over their heads. Some would throw their heads out of the water and make that "br-r-r-r" sound I'd heard earlier; I thought they seemed to be enraged. Then I yanked the lure out of the water towards the vessel and, sure enough, a good-sized Dorado leapt out of the water and nailed the lure in his mouth, growling as he went walking on top of the water! My yank brought the fish to a stop with the lure stuck in his mouth. I threw down the pole and "horsed" my catch on deck, hand-over-hand. The fish fought so valiantly and fiercely on deck that I had trouble holding onto it with both my gloved hands. But I had a fish!

The next attempt brought another Dorado, about the same twelve-pound size as the first, and the third attempt brought one twice as large. I was a fisherman after all! And it was fun! Everytime I swirled the lure around and yanked it out, several angry Dorado would lunge after it and one of them would get hooked! The fish seemed to be whipping themselves into a witless frenzy, hypnotized by my lure that I jerked this way and that before pulling it out of the water to fly into the air. They swam wildly in circles, bumping into each other as they seemed to sharpen their wits for the kill. Often, their jaws would be wide open even as they left the water, teeth bared as they jumped to eat that flying lure. I thought they seemed quite frenetic, so I named my fishing method, "Frenzy Fishing."

I think this kind of fishing is very similar to fly-fishing. All you do is throw the lure into the water, whirl it around, and jerk it out of the water. Then do the same in the opposite direction. The fish go nuts and fight over who will get the lure.

I caught so many that first day that I threw back more than I kept. Ann and I were both ravenously hungry, but I was getting such a thrill out of catching fish that I was giggling! For the first time in my life, fishing was actually *fun*! It was a little sad to watch the brilliantly colored fish fade from their sparkling green, silver, blue and yellow to a dull dead gray, but hunger was stronger than sadness. The best fish dinner I ever had was shortly after I caught my first Dorado with my frenzy fishing method. A dash of lemon juice, a hot frying pan with garlic and butter, and succulent, delicately flavored Dorado steak saved us. What had looked for terrifying hours like a slow voyage to starvation had turned again into another of those wonderful adventures that we'd grown rather accustomed to.

From that first moment on I have never *not* caught a fish when I threw out the lure to use my frenzy fishing method. For the rest of the voyage to Hawaii, Ann and I had fish to eat anytime we wanted. And even when we didn't want, we ate fish. We ate fish and nothing but fish for the rest of the trip. Our menu made for boring meals, but we had food and plenty of it. We ate fish in so many different ways we stopped writing down our new recipes. Fish for breakfast, fish for lunch, fish for dinner, and fish for snacks. Even fish roe—*caviar*—became a drudgery snack.

Today? Well, I don't eat fish if at all possible.

June 29—Working slowly north

We're well into the northeast trades with the wind's blowing a steady force four all night and today. The seas are longer, deeper and more regular than they've yet been since we left the Mexican coast. The *Felucca* easily rolls and amiably pitches in *grande dame* fashion. Breakfast this morning was crisp fish fillet, cooked with salt and limes with a hint of garlic. Delicious.

Here in the trade winds my sensation is one of accomplishment—almost of self-congratulation. I feel certain we will succeed in our voyage to Hawaii and fear has diminished to a mere speck.

To me, the worst part of going to sea is being becalmed. Barely able to endure the slatting and banging, I find that my thoughts too easily turn negative in dead calm seas. The redeeming factor is that there is time to study the sea intimately and enjoy Ann's company while viewing the fish and birds.

Someday I'd like to go aboard a 65-foot schooner (in a moderate breeze like today's) just to feel the difference—if there is any—between its movement and the *Felucca's*. Sir Francis Chichester complained about the "hobby horse" banging motion of his *Gypsy Moth* in moderate to higher breezes, and we have little such movement on the *Felucca*. I thought this 55-foot boat would be relatively stable; however, Chichester's photos show the *Gypsy Moth* heeling at least 35 degrees in small seas. I believe him when he said it was extremely uncomfortable. In his book *Gypsy Moth Circles the Globe*, Chichester says he had a difficult time sailing around the world alone when his self-steering device broke in two and wasn't repairable aboard. Sir Francis then resorted to conventional self-steering sails. He had had experience with this kind of self-steering in the single-handed race he won crossing the Atlantic, relying on a special sail called "Miranda." Chicester tried a similar form of sailing on the *Gypsy Moth IV* but was unable to make it work except with greatly reduced (and slow) storm sails. The fact that *Gypsy Moth IV* could self-steer at all by sail seemed "marvelous" to him. Had he not been able to repair his mechanical Hasler self-steering device, his voyage might have ended in Sydney, Australia. Most sailing cruising vessels will self-steer only in certain directions, so almost all ocean-crossing sailors use a mechanical self-steering device. Otherwise, a larger crew is necessary if hand-steering is needed throughout each twenty-four-hour period.

July 1—Hurricane Denise

I was awakened this morning by the rhythmic rolling of the boat that was heavier than it's been in some time. There is a strong breeze, force six, ranging from 25 to 31 mph. The long, even seas now have white crests on the ridges, some wind streaks on the surface. Our course forces me to quarter the waves so that the *Felucca* rides up one crest and down the other. The wind is now about 30 mph, wheel is lashed amidships, boat surging northwest. I have all sails flying, two large jibs, a main, and a mizzen. This rig will not come into the wind. Every other sailing vessel I know of will come into the wind if the wheel is put at midships, all sails standing in a beam wind. But not my *Felucca!* Her lateen is the perfect sail for crossing an ocean single- or short-handed. In an increased wind, the boat heels about fifteen degrees and her motion becomes more pronounced, but that's about the extent of it. Though she takes an occasional foam-capped sea broadside, there has been no water on deck except for the flecks of spray that blow across. This is unquestionably one of the driest 35-footers I've ever been aboard.

July 2—Getting wilder

Last night the wind came up to 35 mph and I had to douse the main, reducing us to the mizzen and large working jib. We spent an uncomfortable night in the rough, bouncy waves. To alleviate this I moved the mizzen sail to the mainmast (because it's smaller than the main), left the jib in place and ran the small storm sail above the mizzen sail on the mainmast. I call the storm sail a lateen "skysail." It looks fine on top of the mast; the three sails compose a symphony of triangular shapes. The *Felucca* is sailing steadily under my new storm rig in a 35 mph wind from the starboard after quarter. And she's still not heeling more than 15 degrees!

July 3—2000 miles out from Puerto Vallarta

Was a little late this morning on inspection; about 6:30 a.m., however, everything seemed okay. I was disappointed that the wind dropped off a little. Shortly after inspection, I happened to glance aft and saw a new motion on the rudder. The bottom pintle on the rudder at the waterline had broken off! I was stunned. This was totally unexpected or anticipated. The rudder was bending dangerously without the support of all three pintles and gudgeons (those iron pieces that bind it to the stern and let it pivot). There was no possible way of fixing the rudder while it remained in the water. Somehow I had to hoist it on deck, repair the broken part, get it back over the stern and reconnect it to the boat.

We hove to for nine hours. Fixing the rudder wasn't complicated except that I had no new materials to use for repairs; I had to make do with what we had on board. After hoisting the rudder on deck by block and tackle, I unbolted one of the large iron straps which supports the wood. I lit a fire in the galley stove to heat the metal at the appropriate spot. Then I laid the red hot strap on a heavy piece of iron, pounded it into the correct shape, and refitted it in a "jury-rigged" manner to the wood. Then I bolted two 2x6's, one on each side of the rudder, for further lateral support. Though crude, the job was solidly and substantially done. I feel sure that if I can get the rudder back in place, it will hold until we reach Hilo.

We're about 2000 miles out from Puerto Vallarta, so that leaves us about 1,400 miles to go. The loss of the rudder shouldn't be a problem, though. The *Felucca* has steered herself with the wheel lashed for these 2,000 miles, so she ought to be able to continue even if I have to stick an oar back there.

The wind picked up back to a force six breeze. I lowered the rudder into the water with a fourfold purchase tackle, trying five or six times to make the connection. Had I continued trying, I'm sure I would have ruined the rudder. I couldn't get it installed. I decided I couldn't install it until we reached a calm sea or some protected bay. The seas were running rather heavy today so I re-hoisted the rudder back onto the deck. Ann and I went below for a rest. Then I put up the three storm sails I'd been using for the past three days of 30 to 35 mph winds. This is the second time during this ocean crossing that the *Felucca* has sailed with her rudder completely disconnected in a lively breeze. This force six wind remained steady all day slightly ahead of the beam while the ship sailed herself under the storm sails with the rudder safely secured on deck. To give her a little more control, I tied a stout fireman's bucket on a short length of line and let it drag over the after quarter. Immediately, the reaction was almost like giving her a bit of weather helm. The *Felucca* lunged ahead at a steady pace in the wind. As I worked, the wind increased to a force seven level, and the *Felucca* pushed forward as sure-footed as a gazelle! There was a boiling white wake, and our 200-foot lifeline stretched taut behind her. It made its own separate wake in the rising sea. We were running downwind at near surfing speed! With no rudder!

July 4

To celebrate the Fourth of July, we opened our special bottle of Mexican liquor, rice tea, and toasted our friends and families. We played some gin rummy and talked over some of the fun we've had together and spent a fine holiday looking over some of the past and looking forward to the pleasures of the future. My next boat may be an Arab-Indian zaruk, a lateen-rigged gyassa (Nile River cargo carrier), or a Polynesian two-hulled vessel and related lateen rig. I'd like to make the same runs the old-timers did on identical boats without an engine. Ann said that lateen sails must be "my bag." Well, I guess they are.

The wind dropped suddenly today to below a force five, and the ability of the *Felucca* to steer herself with no rudder is considerably reduced. However, I spent an hour adjusting and readjusting the sails to keep her on course without pinching too tightly into the wind. I added a second jib forward, peaked the main lateen as high as it would go, and loosened the sheet's control ropes. These moves put the center of effort forward and caused the vessel to come off the wind to the left. There is now enough control to proceed on a steady course without rudder. I feel reasonably certain that she'll do just fine, but again I say, "We'll see."

We had Ann's version of cerviche today (Mexico's version of sushi: raw fish "cooked" by marinating it in lime juice), then fried fish strips for lunch and tea, then tender white fillets of fish with garlic butter, lemon, and herbs tonight.

Fish, fish, fish.

July 8—Wild winds driving north

We've been sailing along just fine for the last five days with the rudder on deck. I'm finding how well the *Felucca* handles under sail alone. We're heading north by west, pointing 40 degrees to the northeast wind. This is the natural course of the boat with all her sails up. To make her go faster sounds like a crazy wish, but it's true!

The wind is blowing about 35-40 mph today, fifteen degrees ahead of the beam. Layers of dark storm clouds have lingered overhead for the past five days, so I've had only one noon sight during those days . . . rather frustrating. We're lost, technically speaking. Although I'm sure we'll get there, I'm no longer sure where "there" will be. That's one of the nice things about being on the ocean in a seaworthy sailboat; no matter where you are, you can be sure you'll get to land sooner or later if the wind keeps blowing. And the wind we've been having lately gives no sign of letting up!

I believe we have made enough northing to run downwind to Hilo on latitude 20 degrees. At noon I took down the mainsail, put the mizzen sail on the mainmast (because of the mizzen sail's smaller size), and turned the boat to the west. Someday I may sail the *Felucca* to Bali, but I have many reasons for wanting to get her to Hawaii on *this* trip!

We added some variety to our diet tonight: flying fish. We've been eating only those fish my frenzy fishing method has been bringing us, and the high winds and heavy seas brought four of the lightweight fliers on deck by themselves. Their eggs, with a little salt, make a quite acceptable caviar. We called it caviar, even though it was flying fish eggs, plain and simple.

I siphoned the last of the freshwater from our auxilliary 55-gallon drum that's lashed on the starboard foredeck. While I held the hose above, Ann was below in the forepeak filling the jugs inside. The *Felucca* had all storm sails flying and has been careening at a formidable pace. She rises to each oncoming wave, pushing her way up and over into the next one, rolling excessively in the crossseas. Looking back from my seat on the forward hatch, I watch the remaining three-quarters of the boat pitching and swaying like a rollercoaster. At least neither Ann nor I is prone to seasickness!

Later

I remember the day before we planned to leave Monterey to continue our voyage to Mexico, when we added a crew member.

He appeared out of nowhere, attracted by the looks of our boat. A man, accompanied by several people who looked younger than he, came on the dock to look over our boat. He was middle-aged, blue-eyed, slightly long-haired, and was wearing a huge, elegant turquoise ring on his first finger, and his name was Bill. We didn't know it—I don't think he knew it, either—but he was a seasickness candidate. He was a sculptor, and he gave us a beautiful book he had published of photographs of himself and his interesting works. We went with him to visit his studio, located dramatically at the end of Cannery Row overlooking Monterey harbor, and he made no secret of both his admiration of the *Felucca* and his inclination "to go to sea." I thought that we could use another crew member, to stand watches when Ann and I had had enough and to help with deck work, and I thought that this fellow looked strong and intelligent enough. So I asked him.

"Bill," I said, "would you like to take the cruise to Avalon with us? We leave tomorrow. Get your things and come aboard." Avalon is on Santa Catalina Island—not too far away to get to know for sure if Bill could fulfill his apparent potential as a valuable crew member.

Bill thought only for a moment and answered enthusiastically, "I'll go!"

Early that evening, he was aboard with his gear—ready, willing, and apparently able. The next day about noon a friend of his came alongside us in a Monterey fishing boat and towed us out past the point. It wasn't long before we were then sailing merrily off to Avalon.

But there was an unexpected difficulty: the winds were light and from the south. Since we were trying to head south, the only reasonable course we could take was west. We had to head offshore to get sea room instead of trying to beat into the south wind. By the time the wind changed, it was well after nightfall and we were far from shore. With daylight came our preferred north wind, but it made up in force what the previous day's south wind had lacked.

It was a wonderfully hectic sailing day as we bowled southward with all sails flying until, suddenly, near Point Sur, our mainsail yard broke its securing rope, fell overboard, and dragged alongside the boat! Bill and I were grabbing and clawing as we managed to secure it aboard, and we found out soon enough that the parrel had worn through (the parrel is that rope lashing that holds the mainsail to the mast). Then, because of the increasing wind from the north, we continued under only the mizzen sail and jib. We were sailing briskly along well into the night, glorying in the moonlight and marvelling at the phosphorus in the waves. To everyone's surprise, Bill was overcome with seasickness! And then, as if the sail's falling overboard and then Bill's violent stomach hadn't generated enough excitement for one day, the steering apparatus behind the wheel collapsed!

Disabled at sea again. Now it was late at night. The mainsail had to be rerigged as soon as possible, our steering apparatus was fouled up, and our new crew member was seasick in his bunk. With fifteen miles of sea room, the only remaining choice was to throw the sea anchor over the bow. I wanted it to hold us in the same safe area and simply leave the mizzen sail up so we could hove to for the rest of the night. Ann and I then enjoyed a glass of Chablis as she prepared another one of her delicious meals, leading Bill to new and greater spasms of groans and moans while the sweet smells of garlic and butter wafted around the boat. Bill didn't believe me when I assured him that the boat was perfectly seaworthy, was safely hove to, and ready to be repaired completely first thing in the morning. "Let's get a good night's rest because tomorrow we *Travel on to Avalon*." (Al Jolson, 1929.)

That night was uneventful in spite of Bill's ailments and fears. The *Felucca* rode well to her sea anchor while her mizzen sail up had us wallowing and lunging at times, but our fire blazing in our Yukon stove left us warm and—except for Bill—comfortable. And the next morning before anyone else was up, I repaired the steering apparatus and added a new line for hoisting the mainsail. I went up the mainmast to replace the old rope. So we were off and running again when Ann got up, moving sprightly with a fine north wind behind us. We worked our way back nearer shore and had a grand view as we passed Hearst Castle and Point Buchon, but the wind began to drop as we neared Point Arguello. It continued to wane until we found ourselves in a complete flat calm about three miles from Point Conception, one of the most dangerous collections of rocks on the Southern California coast. One of us stayed on watch each hour of the night and made certain we took advantage of each little puff of wind to stay away from the dangers of Point Conception, the Cape Horn of the American Pacific Coast.

The next morning, our fifth since leaving Monterey, Bill was having violent attacks of seasickness; he was looking and feeling worse than ever. I wanted to continue toward San Miguel Island so that we'd reach Santa Catalina as planned, and I sort of argued with him when he asked me to let him off at Santa Barbara. I downplayed the discomfort, saying that it was "only seasickness," and I stressed the pleasures of arriving at Avalon in two or three days. I strongly wanted to avoid having to put ashore at Santa Barbara.

But Bill was insistent. He pleaded, "I'll give you $100 if you'll let me off this boat. Today! I feel like I'm dying, and I want to die on land!"

Hmmmmm, I thought. I was always short on cash, and I was considering his offer.

"I'll write you a check right now. What do you say?" asked Bill.

When I told him I didn't want his check, that I guessed I'd go ahead and try for Santa Barbara, he yanked off his large, hand-made, silver-mounted turquoise ring and cried out, "Please! Here's my ring. For God's sake, please get me off this boat!"

Well, I took the ring and put it on my first finger on my left hand. It fit nicely. Then I lowered the mainsail immediately. We were in a practical calm, anyway, and we'd passed the dangers of Point Conception. It wasn't long before we saw a freighter moving in our general direction, so Ann and I started our system we'd worked out to stop the last freighter: we took down the sails and hoisted the white sheet with the big red X. Ann waved the red pennant, and I blew the SOS signal on the foghorn and the cornet. The freighter changed course, came directly alongside our boat, and offered assistance. I think the entire crew of this Finnish freighter was lined up along her rail in order to gape at the unusual looking American boat with the lateen rig. We explained what was happening, the skipper responded cheerfully, *"Ve vill call de Ghost God,"* and the freighter turned away to her former course. We shouted our thanks and I blew a jazz two-beat tune, "My Blue Heaven," on my cornet.

The Coast Guard came as dependably as it had before. However, this time it arrived with a roar from overhead. The Coast Guard rescue team had come all the way from Los Angeles so that it could hover over us in a helicopter! Its rotor blades were kicking down a tremendous wind, whipping up gusts at least 75 mph. Our sails were on deck, exposed to damage from such a heavy wind. I quickly started trying to secure them so they wouldn't be torn to bits, but I didn't succeed soon enough; the mizzen suffered a 15-foot rip. Two men on the helicopter displayed a blackboard with the chalked message, "Do you need medical assistance?" I relayed a positive answer in as forceful a manner as I could, as Bill, colored green by this time and lying prostrate on deck, confirmed the best he could.

I warned Bill that he'd better be really, really sick because if he wasn't he'd get us all in serious trouble with the Coast Guard. They don't go to this kind of trouble for seasick sailors, I told him. Bill weakly promised to act as sick as he really was and he groaned yet once again to prove his sincerity.

The helicopter men lowered a basket on a thin stainless steel cable amidships, coming in a little lower and increasing the speed of the gale blowing us practically out of the water. I helped poor Bill crawl into the basket, strapped him in with the elaborate safety devices inside, and signaled the pilot to pull him up. But to my horror, instead of taking him straight up, the chopper lurched forward and hauled the basket up right under the shrouds at the head of the mainmast. Bill was in danger of being crushed in the rigging and the *Felucca* was in danger of being dismasted! Ann and I signalled frantically, and they eased down and lowered the basket just in time, dropping Bill with a bone-jarring BANG! back on deck.

By now, Bill had had enough of this rescue effort. He was frantically trying to get himself out of the basket, I was trying to keep the basket's line clear, and Ann was calmly trying to convince Bill to stay in the basket. I signalled the Coast Guard the instant I felt the basket was clear; they pulled straightaway this time, and I could see Bill's hopelessly resigned face as he slowly drifted upwards in the gale that the helicopter's rotors were causing. I never felt so sorry for anyone in my life as I did for poor, green Bill that morning.

It was the next day before I realized that, in all the excitement, I had forgotten to give Bill back his expensive ring.

118

July 9—Storm

The wind blew gale force through the night and increased early this morning to a fresh gale. That wind is strong enough to break large twigs off trees and generally impede progress ashore, and it was driving the seas rather roughly. While wind-streaked fingers are streaming down the concave sections of oncoming waves, the sea is densely flecked with foam everywhere. The rudder is still safely tied on deck, and the *Felucca* steadily rolls and slowly pitches forward gracefully through the gale. An occasional cross sea will hit broadside with a thunderous crash, spray flying and sometimes hitting the deck. When a tremendous roller passes under the boat, I turn to see what it does behind us. It's like looking down from a mountaintop into a deep abyss, the "trough." I'd never have believed that waves could be so high, so deep, and so majestically big, just by hearing someone tell me. But now I've actually seen them. They are great hills of water, constantly moving. The giant waves that have rolled by can be seen at least a quarter of a mile beyond, driving inexorably onward.

July 11—It got worse

The wind has steadily increased! We're in a genuine gale with hurricane-level gusts of 75 mph and slightly more! I hold on and look to the left and see row after row of gigantic waves, stretching to the horizon; I look to the right and see the same thing. It's incredible how high the waves are and how deep are their valleys. The *Felucca* rides each one, up, up, up to the top and whoosh! Down to the bottom and starts up again. I don't know if a rudder would help or not, but she's still steering herself! She's heading downwind under her own steering, surfing in this terrifying sea.

We've been running slightly downwind under two storm sails. I think this is easier than trying to head into the storm in a hove-to position. The sails are made of heavy canvas so nothing has parted (yet?), but the sheets are bar tight. I wanted to keep the ship from going broadside to these mountains of seawater, and she's riding five times easier with her storm sails up than she would just drifting under bare poles! And she's keeping herself on course with no trouble! I was on the verge today of taking down the sails and throwing over the sea anchor, but Ann pointed out how everything was working as it is and said that if it works I shouldn't try to fix it! She's a gutsy lady!

It's easy to sleep below; we're not heeling much at all. But I get up several times to look around. This sea is ominously heavy, and we have no way of getting out of the path of any ship that might bear down on us. The weather is keeping our adrenaline flowing every hour of the day and night, but the solid feel of the *Felucca* keeps it from boiling over into anything resembling panic.

We're both getting to the point where we talk a lot about any food that doesn't have fins or gills.

Later—Glad to get through

We learned in Hawaii that we sailed through Hurricane Denise, a storm that clocked 100 mph winds. My estimate of wind speeds we faced at sea, however, stayed at a maximum of about 75-80 mph. Even with my lower estimate, that's quite a wind.

120

You can get an idea of the force of such a wind if you put your head out of a car window when the car is moving about 76 mph.

If we hadn't had that hurricane to push us back on course, we would have bypassed the Hawaiian Islands completely. And there's no way to tell how much faster it helped us get there.

July 14—850 miles from Hilo

In the past forty-eight hours, we've seen more flying fish than we've seen during the entire crossing. Fifty or more white dots will suddenly swarm from the ocean into the air, flying at least a hundred yards before disappearing again into the water. A breathtaking sight!

Now that we've reached latitude 20, thanks in large part to the mighty winds of the last few days, I ran the spritsail (water sail) out under the bowsprit today. I crawled out to the end of the bowsprit in today's force five wind to reeve a line through the block for the sail. The wind seems to be letting up somewhat.

The ship is running downwind, the northeast trade wind on our after starboard quarter, rudder on deck, balancing with the sails, spritsail, two jibs and lateen storm mainsail. The large mainsail is on deck with the rudder. I'm learning more about the balance of this boat all the time. However, not having a rudder in place worries me and I know the rudder will have to stay on deck until we get to land. Or at least into a dead calm out here (which seems unlikely today, and I'm not about to try it in these seas).

We've been making relatively good time on course now for Hawaii. During the past thousand miles the *Felucca* has been able to run, point, and come about—with no rudder. I suggest that any person with a sailing vessel simulate these circumstances, lashing his/her wheel midships, then running, pointing, and coming about by use of sails alone. Though one might not be able to do all these things alone, and maybe one's boat won't respond well to each, at least the sailor would have a more intimate knowledge of his/her sailing craft. It's my opinion that a Marconi or gaff-rigged sailing vessel cannot make the above-described maneuvers without a rudder even if it's skippered by Joshua Slocum! I'd like very much to go onto a conventional sailing yacht and see if this kind of sailing can be done. After being out here for ten days without a rudder at all, I have more confidence in the *Felucca* than ever before. I can't think of anywhere I'd rather be than in the trade winds, sailing for new ports and looking toward new horizons.

Today's frenzy fishing produced an aku fish at least two and a half feet long. I filleted two thick slabs of red meat off each side and Ann served it with lemon-herb butter. I've had officers in the United States Navy tell me that it's next to impossible to catch a fish at sea, that starvation is a major problem for stranded sailors at sea. Do they know of the "frenzy fishing" method? It hasn't failed me yet. Ann and I are running out of ways to prepare fish and we're more than a little tired of eating the same thing day after day, but we're far from starving now, thanks to "frenzy fishing."

I'd also like to know if the Navy is aware of the tremendous versatility of the lateen sail. I'd like for them to rig one of their own lifeboats with a lateen rigging and let me demonstrate its possibilities for them during competitive tests. If every Navy lifeboat were equipped with lateen rigging and equipment for frenzy fishing, we'd see a drastic reduction in related problems. Every sailor would be safer if s/he knew of these two ideas and how they can be put to constructive use at sea; these ideas will save lives.

Later

I remember thinking somewhere in those days how nice it would be to drop anchor in some idyllic port for a few days, go ashore, eat something besides fish, and visit with some new and perhaps old friends. Ann and I found ourselves reminiscing about details of our crossing as we sailed from the Mexican Naval Base at Magdalia Bay toward Puerto Vallarta. As we sailed south from the naval base area, we veered close to the shore frequently during the daylight. Where we weren't close enough to see with the naked eye, I used my mariner's long telescope to bring things into a visual touching range. We wanted to satisfy our curiosity about what was on the land and we did; we saw miles and miles and miles of nothing but rocks, completely devoid of vegetation.

It was incredible. Much of the coastline in that area seemed like the "devil's playground." The skyline was jagged, sharp and prickly. There were no curved lines, it seemed. There were no waving palm trees as in more tropical climes. It was vividly clear that the Baja California coast is a recently (relatively) cooled lava bed. Only some cacti and bits of brush can grow in this bed of jagged, forbidding rock, and even these hardy pieces of flora look as if they are in constant danger of being overcome by the hot, dry rocks that are everywhere.

There wasn't any room for large sand beaches, and we saw none. The mountains of rocks rose right out of the sea, leaving no space for something as frivolous as a beach. This is the kind of country about which ranchers say, "It takes a hundred acres of this land just to keep one jackrabbit alive." All vessels that sail near these shores—especially sailing vessels without engines—have almost no shelter from high winds; it's a dangerous coast and requires cruising with caution.

Ten miles north of Cabo Falso, near the end of Mexico's Lower California, the wind freshened to about 30 mph. The *Felucca* drives downwind, rising like an elevator—up, up, and up. Then she heads downward, slowly at first and then gaining speed to force away the seas beneath her in smoky white foam. We were taking an exhilarating ride on the wind with the rushing waves beneath us.

Then suddenly we saw what turned into several immaculately smooth sandy beaches. Far in the distance, we could see a huge hotel next to the sea. Coming closer, we saw that it was large, all right, and modern. It overlooked the sea and the jagged high rocks. Through the telescope, we spied the Italian passenger liner *Italia* lying at anchor and noticed several other yachts and what looked like fine resort facilities.

Cabo San Lucas is a pivot point for wind, tide, and current. We'd just been in a force six wind, but here, just ten miles away near the cape near Cabo San Lucas, there wasn't a breath of air. There was absolutely no wind but the sea was high and confused. The great surges were crashing into large waves and we couldn't be sure which way the current was going simply by looking at the water. Our yards began banging furiously against the masts, so I lowered them. A calm wind with a rough sea is not a tranquil thing and is frustrating to experience. A high sea isn't really a bother for a sailing ship so long as she has wind in her sails. After all, it's wind that steadies the motion of a sailing vessel. Sails are to the ship as wings are to an airplane. But ours were pandemonium. The sails hung loosely, the yards were slapping back and forth and whacking against the masts with every roll. In this kind of calm that's not calm, there is a constant imbalance.

We had planned to sail into Cabo San Lucas to visit some friends, but there was no wind we could ride to go in. And since we had no engine, we had to sit tight and roll with the waves. We went below and almost immediately heard a ship's horn close by.

I ran up the ladder to discover a handsome 75-foot power yacht, the *Dolly* from Newport Beach, alongside. The skipper shouted, "Are you folks in trouble? Are you all right?"

"Things are fine. We're just waiting on some wind," I shouted back to him.

He laughed and threw us a couple of ice cold beers as he turned course and left us. During this calm, one other power boat and one sailboat came close by to hail us and assure themselves that we needed no help, that things were okay. It became obvious to us after the second offer for help that we must have looked as if we *were* in trouble! But this time we were not in trouble at all.

Three years later in Sausalito, I was casually showing pictures at a party aboard a funky houseboat, and handsome Tom Lloyd suddenly exclaimed, "Hey, I saw that boat off Cabo San Lucas a few months ago! I thought it had escaped from Disney or Peter Pan! I couldn't believe it. There was no one at the wheel and it was sailing along very slowly in an almost dead calm. We circled it several times. I remember calling out only once, and I didn't yell very loud. We figured you didn't want to be disturbed. A fishing pole was erect on the afterdeck, trailing a line. Three sails were up and the vessel proceeding at about 1 mph. It looked like you guys really had it together! I'll never forget seeing that boat out there on those waters!" I thanked him, belatedly, three years later in Sausalito.

Finally a breeze came from the west, giving us some favorable wind for a run to Mazatlan. We put up the main and mizzen lateen sails in the "St. James Cross" position. That's where the yard is positioned to form a cross with the mast. Yanko Varda of Sausalito used to call it, "the Cr-r-r-ross of St. James." With that breeze and those sails, we began our voyage across the Sea of Cortez.

A day later the wind veered slightly. Ann and I talked it over: Getting to Mazatlan on that slant this new wind was giving us would be very difficult, but, as Ann pointed out once again, we had no schedule. We had no commitment to go to Mazatlan, so it wasn't all that problematic to decide simply to continue on the tack we had established comfortably with the wind we had. We referred to our Mexican AAA road map and concluded that the island we were watching on the southeast horizon had to be the northernmost of the Isles Marias. That begins an island group that is midway between Mazatlan and Puerto Vallarta, and Ann voiced the thought we had both only sort of decided: "T. Jay, why don't we just skip Mazatlan and head for P.V.?" Our new course was charted.

While we were gliding past the islands, several small open native fishing boats changed course out of curiosity and came alongside to inspect our boat. We invited two fishermen aboard for a cup of coffee. One of the men told us (in English) exactly where we were; San Blas and Puerto Vallarta were fifty and one hundred miles away, respectively, and when they left us they took two letters to mail for us in San Blas (we were changing our forwarding address from Mazatlan to Puerto Vallarta).

These men fished for shark, taking a long line with up to seventy-five shark-baited hooks and weighting it so that it would sink to the bottom. Sometimes they would draw on this line as many as twenty-five small sharks, averaging about five feet long, at a time. These sharks were used almost entirely; there was almost no waste. Their skins make a rough fabric, their meat was sold for human consumption, and the remainder of the fish was sold for bait. I took a silent pleasure in knowing that these fishermen were taking sharks by the hundreds everyday. I don't think I'll ever get over my irrational fear of sharks.

Sailing in light winds, we eventually entered Banderas Bay and began the countdown sail into Puerto Vallarta. We sailed into P.V. about midnight under a brilliant full moon that was brighter than the bright Punta Mita harbor light. Even though it was almost as bright as day, however, I was not going back on my solemn promise to stay on watch as we neared land. It will take a long time for that memory of being a castaway to recede and become less vivid.

About 3:00 a.m. the wind died completely, and we drifted quietly in the setting moon's still bright light, in the morning's breaking, and until about noon. Then, a strong westerly sprang up. Then it was only a short time before we began to see buildings in the distance, with smoke and signs of the town. We put up all our sails including the Mexican-colored jib (green, red, and white) and paraded down the shore past private homes, native huts, and bright, white hotels. We could see the central church tower and thought it looked like a crown that rested easily on the head of what was the old part of Puerto Vallarta. Mansions and huts alike cling to the precipitous hillsides behind the town, and we watched many of them with people coming outside to watch us. The coconut palms, bamboo, and profuse vegetation of all kinds were lush and splashed with brilliantly colored flowers, giving us welcome changes from the starkly vacant rock of just a few miles up the coast. We had arrived in Puerto Vallarta.

July 15—Rudder back on at sea

I was dismayed by the noon sight; we've made only 120 miles in the last two days. We were making good a course of northwest by west but had to change to due west. Sailing without a rudder for over a thousand miles has been educational, to say the least, but I can no longer amble along under just the storm rig. The time has come to remount the rudder. I can tack without it, but with the rudder in place I can put up the mainsail and make a beeline for Hilo at twice the speed we're now maintaining. Ann and I decided that we'll try to put the rudder as soon as the wind slacks. We should do this job in a calm harbor; installing it in a force three wind will be difficult. If I fail, we could really be up against it in an emergency because we'll soon be well into the shipping lanes. I just can't fail!

July 16—Back to latitude 20

Replacing the rudder and getting it working again was one helluva feat! I tried to plan with utmost care every single step we were to take. The rudder itself is cumbersome and heavy, even for two strong men to handle alongside a dock in quiet water. It's just Ann and me out here in the open sea, and we had a 12–15 mph wind for our task; the ship lurched and occasionally did flick rolls—usually at the precise moment we were about to align something. I hoisted the rudder with a fourfold purchase tackle from the top of the mizzenmast and made a special small boom to hold the tackle over the stern directly in line with the gudgeons. I attached a preventer running from the end of the boomkin back to the rudder itself so that I could pull the rudder back, if necessary, to align the pintles with the gudgeons.

From the Jacob's ladder, hanging on the boomkin and handling the rudder to align it, I swung like a monkey on a vine. When a larger than usual wave overtook us, I'd be submerged to my neck in the water. I had a fish-eye view of the *Felucca* as it seemed to descend upon me. With a piece of manila line I lashed the bottom pintle to its gudgeon and lined up the other two above. Ann and I were able, by making adjustments with tackle and preventer, to insert the long bar that holds it together so that it slid through all three holes to secure the rudder to the boat.

While I was on the ladder in the sea with boat heaving and rudder tossing about in midair, a hopeless feeling overwhelmed me for a moment. I felt beaten by the apparent futility of struggling with a job too big for us in such a vast expanse of unsettled water. But I kept working down in the water. By some miracle, we completed the task and got the rudder back where it belongs. With Ann's help, I got the job done. So for the rest of the day and tonight, we're off and running in the 15 mph trade wind, heading on a true course for Hilo.

July 17—800 miles from Hilo

We've had to "beat" upwind from Mexico to within 800 miles of Hawaii. We finally made northing to latitude 20, time to turn due west. The *Felucca* steered herself all the way and continues to do so, wheel lashed, running almost straight downwind. During the coast cruise from Sausalito to Puerto Vallarta, I wasn't able to get the boat to steer herself when sailing straight or near downwind. I thought this was a permanent quirk of the lateen

I'd have to learn to live with. I've found during this crossing that she'll self-steer herself downwind quite easily. I've had many months of sailing with lateen sails and have discovered these gratifying characteristics. I'm a solid devotee of them now, with a firm base of reason for that devotion, because of the ease with which we're able to cross this part of the Pacific.

The pleasure is long gone from catching fish. As pleased as I am that my frenzy fishing method is so reliable, I'd give all the fish in the ocean right now for one ear of corn on the cob with a T-bone steak.

Even fish eggs have lost all appeal for me. Calling it caviar doesn't even help anymore. We've had "caviar" to eat almost everyday now for a while. Caviar and fish. Fish and caviar.

July 18—Near Hawaii

This is the 51st day of our voyage out of Mexico. Each day seems shorter and shorter. After being at sea for a long time, I fully expected to be a little stir crazy. Not so. Even though it's high time we should be in Hawaii, I don't mind at all, looking forward to its taking several more days yet. The downwind rig of spritsail, main lateen and jib are running to my satisfaction, and I don't change the wheel setting unless the wind velocity changes drastically. So it goes and so it has gone for days at a time.

Later

Ann and I, once again, slipped into reminiscing about Our Trip, the easy way it started and how we had enjoyed it so, even when it wasn't going quite the way we'd expected or wished. We both had many, many pleasurable memories of Puerto Vallarta, and that night we exchanged and compared them lovingly. Puerto Vallarta, one of the loveliest towns in all of Mexico, has been a popular vacation spot for Mexicans for years and has been "discovered" by international tourists now as well. It has a delightful combination of palm-covered hills, interesting architecture, white sand beaches, cobblestone streets, and a small river running through it. The many small shops offer a wide variety of things that one would ordinarily have to rummage around for all over the country, things like leather and woven goods and wrought iron articles both for artistic enjoyment as well as practical uses. Since it is somewhat of a mecca for tourists, prices are generally higher there than elsewhere in Mexico.

There are also many restaurants and bars. We especially enjoy the sidewalk-vendor taco stands where we frequently feasted on fresh tacos—varying our choices among beef, pork, steer's head, and tripe on a hot soft taco with toppings of chopped onions, cilantro, salt, and spicy sauce—for only one or two pesos each. We have no difficulty with the water in P.V., drinking freely from a tap at a gas station or a hotel or the spigot at the marina. I think it's not the water (or even the food) that causes so may typical tourists to develop "Montezuma's Revenge"; I think it's the flies. There aren't unusually great numbers of flies there, but they do exist; they alight on open sewage then wing their way uptown to where all the people (and more garbage) are. Then they traipse around over the food and sometimes the glassware people drink from, tracking that germ or virus or whatever it is that causes the "two-step" everywhere they go. When the same two people go everywhere together in Mexico and eat and drink the same foods and liquids and only one of them gets the bug, it's hard to believe that the bug's only "in the water."

At low tide everyday, native men go to the beach to pick up loads of smooth, round stones. Each man brings several burros with gunny sacks slung over their backs for the stones and makes several trips from beach back to town. Then the artisans and craftspeople use the stones for cobblestone street paving, to make fences, to cover paths, and to do a number of other useful things with those stones that washed up free from the sea on their beach. Native women tend to prefer the Rio Cuale, a small river with fresh warm water that runs through the older part of town, as they take care of their laundry chores. Nature provides all they need for a complete wash except the soap. We watched women slap their clothes on large, flat smooth rocks, scrub and rinse them in the wide braided streams among an ample number of rocks, and then hang them on bushes and rocks to dry. We tried this a few times and found that our clothes smelled fresher and looked cleaner than when we used the ordinary washing machines! Unfortunately, each year the Rio Cuale gets more and more polluted, and it's unlikely that nature's laundromat in Puerto Vallarta can continue much longer.

And like anyplace with a collection of diverse and interesting people, Puerto Vallarta's architecture is quite interesting. It includes everything from the simplest of thatched huts to meticulously manicured and landscaped mansions that pose as haciendas, and sometimes the two extremes can be found on the same part of the same street. The attractively designed ordinary houses, very different from those in the United States, are consistently individual; each is an original design that doesn't look like any other in town; some are plain, but each is invigorating simply to look at.

We visited people in several homes while we were there, and one delightful visit inside a remarkable piece of architecture was in a house that was designed and built by one of the local architects. It had three levels and spacious common areas. Fireplaces were everywhere, including a giant one in one of the four bedrooms. Just outside the rear deck, a noisy little brook ran past, tumbling down a landscaped ravine. An arched stone bridge over a waterfall connected the deck with the barbecue terrace. The house seemed to be basically a Spanish Renaissance style with adobe blocks, heavy-beamed ceilings, tile floors, curved red tile roofing, latticed open areas, enormous fireplaces, and extensive brick and stonework by master workmen. It's located on two hillside acres with a panoramic view of Banderas Bay. This house was completed for less than $60,000 (including the cost of the land!); in the United States, that money probably wouldn't have been able to buy even the two acres.

One of the very first things I did upon arrival in P.V. was to begin searching for a skiff to replace that last one I'd lost at sea. I discovered right away that a conventional U.S. type of dinghy or skiff was impossible to find. These small craft disappeared immediately from vendors' stocks just as quickly as they could be put out for sale, and they almost never appeared in the first place. I had admired the craft that natives used to swoop through the surf without taking in a drop of water, having closely inspected a few *canoas* in some detail. I'd found that they are simply dug out of single logs and then, perhaps, painted or oiled and

130

decorated. I found one for sale without too much difficulty and bought it for $40. We named it *"Chiquito,"* or "little one."

When we first tried the *Chiquito* and tried going through the surf, we found that it was topheavy and tender; it almost tipped over if we merely leaned to one side. So we put on our bathing suits and experimented. We found that the "secret" was simply to sit flat on the bottom. That brought the center of gravity of the little ten-foot skiff down, and the result was a steadying force. After some practice, I had learned how to paddle through the heavy surf and take on only a small amount of spray and a few drops of water off the paddle. After we learned how to use it to our best advantage, it turned out to be a remarkably stable and useful ship-to-shore skiff.

One evening when we were invited to a dinner party ashore, Ann went with ten or so friends down to the pier to watch me take the *canoa* through the surf from the *Felucca*. I saw them as I embarked, and I waved at them confidently. Just as I waved, however, I felt a sudden huge surge and looked over my shoulder to see one of the largest waves I'd yet seen in this heavy surf! It was a "ninth wave" rushing toward me! While I held my paddle at the ready, the *canoa* reared up by the stern to a 45-degree angle and then shot down the face of the big wave through the white comber on top. Somehow, I managed to keep balanced and took the little craft right up to the high watermark on the beach as my small audience of onlookers applauded.

A friend from a nearby large yacht lost his small skiff as he tried to row in through the pounding surf one day. His skiff broached to in the waves and broke into four large pieces and was washed onto the beach. I saw no such broken *canoas*. Another acquaintance broke his leg trying to take his skiff through the breakers. We found why the local residents preferred the *canoa* with its paddle; it could ride the surf like a surfboard. We painted our little *canoa* in the same colors as the *Felucca* and began to look forward to taking it through the surf in other places as well.

We met so many wonderful people while there. One afternoon on the beach, Ann met an elderly captain who had retired from his lifelong profession as a St. Lawrence Riverway pilot. In his wonderfully thick French-Canadian accent, he asked her if he could come aboard to visit us, and he came promptly. The following noon he arrived with a friend from Montreal and was loaded with several bottles of beer, tequila, and mixer. We enjoyed two delightful cocktail hours exchanging sea stories and snapping photographs of each other.

On the beach another day, we met a widower named Marc Bradford. He was in his early seventies and was resplendent with his headful of thick white hair and Papa Hemingway beard. He was a world traveller, having recently arrived in Puerto Vallarta from Pago Pago enroute to Mexico City and then to Costa Rica and on to Miami. He travels around the world alone, "searching," as he says, "but not quite finding." I don't envy his going it alone; I prefer going with my lovely Ann, moving forward together, sharing, studying the same star. Each person we met was so filled with the exuberance of life that I think each and every one could easily be the basis for a whole series of exciting stories.

We truly enjoyed our stay, but it wasn't all "beer and skittles," to be sure. We faced some serious problems from the moment we dropped anchor. A big problem was no money and no word as to when it would arrive even though we expected it would be waiting for us when we came. I had had to call to the sailboat the *White Cloud* that was anchored near us and get Mike Woods, her skipper, to row us ashore, since we had lost our skiff at that point. We had rushed to the post office, but the anticipated mail with our checks was not there. We walked a mile along the waterfront everyday for a month to the post office looking for that mail. During that month, the few pennies we did have disappeared, so there we were without money, passports, skiff, or second anchor in a foreign port. I didn't know then what I know now about fishing, so "food" in my mind still was automatically equated with "money."

We didn't go hungry, but we were reduced from Ann's regular culinary delights to ordinary rice and beans with an occasional fish a friend would bestow on us. Other cruisers we met were generally sympathetic and helpful. It's frightening to be out of money in a foreign country, and it was a first time for both Ann and me. After a month of no mail, I wired relatives and got a few extra dollars. That let us buy the *canoa* and pay off the few debts we'd incurred, and it made waiting for the mail a little easier.

Because I had no papers, I was afraid to go to the Port Captain for assistance. I knew there would be a fine, and I couldn't afford to pay for food, let alone pay for a fine. I'd heard the horror stories that if one gets into trouble in Mexico without funds to get one out, one is in deep stuff. Day after day we thought, "The money will be here tomorrow," and we'd plan to get our supplies and sail on to Acapulco. We thought we'd get the proper papers in Acapulco so that we could become legal Mexican visitors, but the money didn't come.

After resting at anchor for two months, a powerful motorboat with markings from Mexican officialdom and crew members who looked just as official as the boat pulled up alongside the *Felucca*. My heart sank. I knew they were finally after me. One of the officials tapped on the side of the *Felucca* and shouted, "Mr. Rockford, we want to talk with you."

Good grief! They even knew my name! Visions of dark, dank Mexican jails rushed through my head as I invited him aboard as calmly as I could.

A clean-shaven, slightly overweight man clambered up our Jacob's ladder. Even though we exchanged appropriate cordialities and amenities—and drank Ann's delicious coffee—he didn't drop his heavily officialized bearing and way of speaking. He asked questions formally in a sibilant voice and wrote my answers on his legal-sized tablet. He asked how long had I been in Mexico, what was my first port of entry, why was I in Puerto Vallarta, how come I hadn't left yet, how come I hadn't reported to the Port Captain's office upon arrival, etc., etc., etc. I tried to tell him the truth and I knew that each of my answers was getting me in deeper trouble with this representative of the Mexican Government, and his attitude was growing more and more skeptical. He got to where he looked as if he didn't believe one word I was saying.

"Mr. Rockford," he intoned with a definite chill, "we're going to have to take you into the marina. We want you to be ready to leave in two hours."

He bade us a brief, terse farewell, and exactly two hours later we were under tow from the Port Captain's official tugboat. People we'd met as well as people we hadn't met yet came to their rails to watch in amazement. We were the first vessel I'd seen in two months that had the formality of a visit by such officialdom, let alone officialdom's major tugboat towing a vessel into the marina. I tried to joke and shouted to the onlookers that it was probably only some kind of "house arrest." I didn't want any of them to know that I was certain we would spend the next few years in Puerto Vallarta's Mexican jail.

I expected the tug to put us with the other tourist vessels that predominated in the marina. It's a safe harbor with modern facilities and a new terminal building for port officials, and it's almost always bustling with many visiting boats that seem always to be coming or going. Instead of putting us there, however, the tug towed us past the visible parts, past the fine yachts and visiting vessels, and tied us next to a couple of workboats on a mud flat hidden from casual view. Within twenty minutes of tie-up, every boating person in the Bay knew we had been towed in by the Port Captain. Two captains we knew came over within minutes and cheered us up, helping us to laugh about our predicament.

That was the night when Dave Brooks from Sausalito surprised us, coming by with his friend Lou. When we explained our problems with the Port Captain, Dave offered me several bits of advice. His main point was that I should wear the captain's hat he'd noticed on my head during the tow earlier when I kept the 3:00 p.m. appointment to see the Port Captain later on this afternoon.

"The Mexicans will have much more respect for you with that hat on. In fact, I want to borrow it right now," he said. "My crew member Bob was arrested and jailed last night. I need your captain's hat because I want to go down there and get him out."

I was incredulous. A *hat* has that much influence? Dave believed it did, so we traded hats. I let him wear my captain's hat and he gave me his Panama with the multicolored hatband. By golly, his appearance changed considerably, and he *did* look significantly more official! He looked commanding, slightly fiercer than before, and definitely important. When he returned later that day with his just-imprisoned crew member, I was fully convinced beyond a shadow of a doubt that I would wear that captain's hat to see the Port Captain. And, for better or for worse, I've worn one constantly since then.

At 3:00 p.m., I was in the waiting area of the Port Captain's office, hat definitely not in hand, but firmly on my head in the most intimidating position I could find for it. I hadn't slept at all that night before, and I was half sick with worry. I'd just spoken with a young bearded Texan who hadn't had the proper papers and who'd been fined $500 and had received his deportation order; he'd lost his boat, too. I'd convinced myself that I'd be fined $500 and that I couldn't pay it. The Port Captain would impound my boat, too, and then deport both of us. Three lackeys almost jumped to attention and saluted when I walked in. The same official who had come aboard to ask the questions was there; he greeted me politely and asked me to be seated.

It was the official who took me into the Port Captain's office and actually conducted the business of our meeting. It was just the two of us. He was very polite but he got to his point, very, very slowly. It took him a very long time to speak this statement, "Mr. Rockford, we're going to have to fine you."

I said something about my boat's being so special, about how I had no money but "the check was in the mail, ha ha ha," but he didn't appreciate the joke. He was quite serious.

"We have to fine you. The fine is fifty dollars U.S.," he finally said.

"Fifty dollars!" I blurted out. I was amazed with relief that it wasn't $500!

"All right, I can reduce it to forty dollars, but no more," the official said. I wasn't trying to bargain with him, but I think he thought I was.

"I don't have the money, as I told you. But in a few days I will and then I can pay you. Will that be acceptable?" I was trying hard not to reveal how relieved I was.

He agreed to my request for a delayed payment and placed us under "house arrest" until we paid the fine. I tried to borrow the $40 from several people that evening, but was unsuccessful. One would-be lender was a divorcee we'd met. She'd been telling us how much she was enjoying spending money here in Mexico, and she'd given the clear impression that she had enough cash to loan someone $40 if they would but ask. However, she confided in me that she was broke, that she was staying in Puerto Vallarta because she didn't have the money to leave. I remember that her story made me think, involuntarily, of an old jazz piece I play, "Nobody Loves You When You're Down and Out."

While Ann and I were discussing what to do about the $40, we decided to continue Our Trip by sailing across to Hawaii and leave Puerto Vallarta. We wanted the fine weather, but we also wanted to get back into the United States; it was much easier there to get "money from home." Mexican fishermen and seasoned mariners had warned us not to head west now because it would be a particularly dangerous journey at this time of year. At any-time, they said, the Santa Ana winds can be killers, but those winds and their bigger brothers the hurricanes are especially rampant in late summer. However, Ann and I were eager to be on the open sea again, and Hawaii was sending its siren song. We decided to leave as soon as possible after our checks came, regardless of these warnings about the weather.

At last the checks arrived. We bought canvas to make a new mainsail, we paid off the $40 fine, and we restocked the boat with food and supplies. Our friend Don from the television station dropped by from San Diego, bringing some supplies and useful items unavailable in Puerto Vallarta, and he stayed with us about a week. Unfortunately, Don contracted "Montezuma's Revenge" and was extremely ill. The illness even affected his mind at times. When he was leaving us to return to the States, he was carrying his suitcase in one hand and his hat in the other. He stepped out of the *canoa* next to the dock, but calmly walked into the water instead of onto the dock. He sank like a stone into eight feet of water while his suitcase and hat floated without him. Happily, he wasn't injured at all and joined us in laughing at what seemed at the time like a scene from a Laurel and Hardy movie.

We moved from the mud flat to a sand beach in the harbor near the marina where Don, Ann and I scraped and painted the hulls of the *Felucca* and our *canoa*, the *Chiquito*, at low tides. Everyone in the Marina seemed to share our delight in watching the *Felucca* perk up with its new white mainsail and neat new coats of paint, gleaming black with yellow boot topping ten inches above the waterline. We moved into high gear in preparation for going across the Pacific to Hawaii.

Only a few days after Don's departure, we were being towed from the marina to Yelapa near the mouth of the bay; we were getting under way again! Captain Gordon Balzarett agreed to tow us out in his *Sea Nymph*, a 45-foot motor yacht. This was a special courtesy that we greatly appreciated because working the *Felucca* out of a bay directly against the wind presents almost insurmountable problems. This same problem was faced by the old-time sailing ships, of course, in the days before engines, but they simply waited for more favorable winds; we were ready to go and didn't want to wait a day longer than we had to!

Pennants and flags flew from every possible point on the *Felucca*. Ann had even sewn me a new Corinthian Yacht Club flag and had designed two new flags: a Libra and a Leo horoscope symbol for her and for me, and these were flying too. The image must have been wonderful for the onlookers: an immaculate white motor yacht pulling our freshly painted, historic-looking black vessel out to sea, and I was belting out "I Left My Heart in San Francisco" on my antique cornet. Crews and captains from most of the boats in the marina and the harbor came up topside to cheer, to take photographs, and to wave farewell. We had spent several lovely months in Puerto Vallarta, but it was time to sail again. With God's help, we were headed for Hawaii!

July 19—2,000 miles at sea; drink seawater

One doesn't *have* to go into the high seas to find solitude or to enjoy seclusion. Though those two special places of mind and heart are difficult to find they're possible on a boat anywhere. San Francisco Bay, Chesapeake Bay, Puget Sound, the Mississippi River . . . even 2,000 miles at sea. All one needs to do is up anchor and sail to a quiet cove off the beaten track. Houses built for seclusion are too soon surrounded by other houses. When one throws a bucket of slop off one's back porch, there's no privacy if it hits a neighbor's house next door. Privacy tends to vanish everywhere on land. Most people on land can *never* get away from their telephones, their unneeded visitors, their irrelevancies and time-wasters. Amid large populations, it's possible to escape the constant hubbub, the barking of dogs, the yelling of people, loud noises next door, sounds of autos, trucks, police and fire sirens, the garbagemen at 4:00 a.m., hot rods and squealing tires at all hours of the night.

There's really none of that on the water. On a boat, the world offers endless miles of bays, rivers, oceans, and bayous where one can still find peace, privacy, and Paradise.

I started drinking seawater a couple of days ago. Our freshwater supply won't last but a few more days, and I want to be sure there's enough for Ann. She refuses to drink seawater and warns me that she'll force freshwater down my throat if I start making arrangements to cook her up for dinner! Actually, I don't "guzzle" it. I take no more than about a cupful in twenty-four hours. It takes away the thirst, and the only side effect that I've noticed is somewhat loose bowels.

July 20—Fountain of youth

Solitude is enlarged ten times over on a transoceanic crossing. I value my solitude highly. Some famous thinker/writer wrote somewhere that a man who likes solitude is either a beast or a god. I don't really care which he would classify me as being, but I find solitude to be nourishing and peace-giving. By "solitude," I don't mean being alone. I don't think I could have enjoyed this crossing anywhere near the way I have if Ann hadn't been with me; loneliness is not for me, but solitude is. When I want it, I need it and revel in it.

Solitude helps me clear my mind of incidentals, and my thinking on any subject is broadened and more focused. New details come to me that I hadn't thought of before. Getting away from the bustle of modern civilization and machinery has given my mind an added dimension, I think. Surely everyone should "get away from it all" at least once a year in idyllic seclusion. Isn't that what Catholics call a "retreat"? I guess the idea for solitude as sort of panacea is as old as humanity because various forms of it have been sought after for generation after generation. I heartily endorse the idea.

My very attitude toward life itself has changed profoundly as a result of "getting off the treadmill" and by this particular crossing. After two years of sailing and living aboard the *Frisco Felucca II*, my health is excellent, and my weight has returned to the same as it was when I graduated from college thirty years ago. I'm physically stronger than I've ever been, and the emotional crises that consistently overwhelmed me in the past, sometimes for days or weeks, have almost ceased to occur. I'm inclined to believe that perhaps I've discovered what Ponce de Leon was searching for, the elusive fountain of youth.

Later

Before those July days of meditating on the value I place on solitude, Ann and I both had discussed how we enjoyed it and how we found it so rejuvenating. We enjoy people very much, but that's not the point. For example, when we had seen our seasick passenger, Bill, leave in his helicopter basket, Bill had been with us less than a week—and had been mostly out of sight with his savage attack of seasickness. But Ann and I were acutely aware of our solitude within minutes after he left. Halfway between Point Conception and San Miguel Island on our way to Avalon, we were alone together again. At the time, the episode with Bill was terrifying; both his life and my boat were in serious jeopardy. The Coast Guard had come to the rescue once again, offering their great machines where needed, and we were too frightened and too thankful for their assistance to carp about their particular methods of rescue.

But we were back on course. The weather stayed easy for the next twenty-four hours, giving us a chance to look at each detail of the day and night and to savor the peacefulness of the experience. During that night, we slowly passed San Miguel Island, approaching Santa Rosa Island. The very atmosphere underwent a complete change in feeling and appearance when we entered the Santa Barbara Channel Islands. We spotted several sharks—our first—swimming near the boat. We saw untold numbers and kinds of fish in the crystal clear water. And we were fascinated by the abundance of phosphorescence in the water that burst into light at the slightest provocation. We'd only been under way for a few days and had had more than our share of difficulties, I thought. We'd already been through almost all kinds of weather, we'd lost our rudder, we'd had two Coast Guard rescues, we'd suffered a ripped sail and a fire aboard, our mainsail had collapsed and our steering apparatus had failed; now I felt we'd had our disasters and nothing more could happen. We were now thoroughly enjoying our all-but-perfect sailing.

Actually, it was too close to perfect, and I began to wish for some stiffer wind so we could learn more about what to do in a blow with our lateen-rigged vessel. My wish was secret, but early the next morning, here came the wind! After our restful and beautiful day and night of picture-book sailing, the wind began blowing with a vengeance, reaching a force six level within an hour. This time, I mounted the storm sail on the mainmast and put a small jib ahead of it; for the next eight hours at least, it was "Ride 'em cowboy!" With the slack taken out of her steering device, the *Felucca* responded well to her new, larger rudder. Using less canvas than necessary—rather than being over-canvassed in such a powerful wind—gave us all the control we needed. The boat would rush down each overtaking wave and vigorously climb the steep side of the next one, throwing spray from both sides of the bow and yawing only imperceptibly. It was exciting and we loved it. I remember thinking that it felt like the *Felucca* was loving the excitement, too. I realized that the three of us were gaining more and more confidence in her: Ann and I and the *Felucca* herself.

The boat steered herself on all courses with the wheel lashed, particularly in moderate winds. Ann and I took full advantage of this miraculous self-steering ability and stood two-hour watches after 10 p.m., giving each of us a full uninterrupted two hours of sleep off watch. Standing watch consisted mainly of sitting below in front of the glowing fireplace, drinking coffee and glancing occasionally at the small hand compass we had in order to be certain that we hadn't fallen off course. Every fifteen minutes or so, the helmsman would go on deck to look carefully around the horizon to check for other vessels that might be nearby. But most of the watch time was spent reading a good book; it was an easy routine.

If the wind was blowing hard and we were running downwind, the boat had to be steered constantly. But if we had a broad reach or if we were sailing close to the wind, the *Felucca*, with wheel lashed, would steer herself for hours.

Another day of calm came upon us and we slowly passed Santa Barbara Island. In the afternoon, two red jet fighter planes swooped low over the water and waved in passing. Herb couldn't have relayed the news of our coming to his colleagues in jet fighters this far south, so we figured that our unusual Columbus-like sailboat was simply irresistible to those in their modern jet airplanes.

Santa Catalina Island remained our goal and remained hidden in the morning mist. It was in sight from the first moment we could make it out in the distance. But almost as soon as we spotted it, the wind collapsed. It simply disappeared. It took a full day of beating to get to Avalon Harbor, and it was almost midnight when we finally dropped the hook in front of the famous old Avalon Ballroom. We had made it all this way without an engine!

We'd used nothing but sails! And I'd learned a great deal about how to sail a lateen-rigged vessel on the high seas.

We stayed in Avalon seven days, meeting and being entertained by several fine people. We telephoned Chuck Rogers (the news photographer from Channel 13, back home), to let him know we'd made it successfully through the first leg of Our Trip, and we called our parents too. Their reactions combined relief with excitement. They all expressed grateful amazement that we'd made it, alive and breathing quite well, thank you, in the *Frisco Felucca II*. Chuck tried to rework his schedule to come to San Diego to get some more television footage but failed, so we decided to sail on directly from Avalon to Ensenada, Mexico.

I remember how the night before Christmas Eve we took advantage of a favorable late evening wind and hoisted anchor. We sailed gently out of Avalon in a quiet, moonlit night. However, we got only about a mile out and, once again, the wind died suddenly and we started drifting back toward the rocky beach. I cursed, fortified myself against the chilly moonlight with a long swig of Ann's special red wine, climbed into the skiff, attached a long line to the stemhead of the *Felucca*, and rowed. I towed the *Felucca* clear of Santa Catalina Island, inspired frequently to row harder by the phosphorescent spray of breakers on the rocks near the beach and by the roar of the nearby surf. I really leaned on those oars for at least an hour, but I got us clear. At some point, the wind picked up a little, turned warm, and seemed steady enough for me to lash the wheel. The *Felucca* steered herself the rest of the night, heading herself and us towards Mexico in the way people dream of sailing to Mexico.

Christmas Eve saw us sailing past San Diego. We were making slow progress in the mild winds, but everything we saw was interesting territory for us and we didn't mind our pace. We stayed about five miles offshore and kept excellent visibility in the crisp winter air. That night, Ann prepared a special fettucine dinner, complete with fine wine and candlelight, cozy fireplace ablaze, and the *Felucca* tending to her own steering. I played Christmas carols on my old-fashioned horn, and we watched for Santa Claus in the clear skies as the holiday lights of San Diego twinkled at us in passing.

Christmas day, Ann woke me excitedly. "T. Jay, come back on

deck and look! We're in Mexico! I see Table Mountain! Come look at the gorgeous sunrise!"

I went above before dressing and drank in the wonderful sight. We were in Mexico indeed, and the very heavens themselves were laying out their finest raiments to welcome us. We had no charts for the waters south of the United States, but I wasn't worried. Yes, we'd have to observe the coastline carefully as we progressed, but I'd been in Todos Santos Bay before and knew it wasn't complicated, and the winds were cooperating with a light breeze.

Early the next day, I was doing light deck work when I heard a loud, breathy noise over my right shoulder. I glanced up and saw a gigantic, dark gray shape at least 35 feet long in the water about 50 yards or so from the *Felucca*. It was a whale! I shouted for Ann to come and look as the great creature moved forward and upward. Its tremendously large tail rose vertically into the air as the mammal sounded.

There were light gray spots on its back which I thought were barnacles, and I had a funny feeling in my stomach: awe, respect, and fear. All at once.

That day, just as we neared Ensenada, Ann decided I should catch a fish for dinner. I hated fishing, but I agreed with her that we needed a varied diet. After all, Chuck Rogers had given me a pole, tackle and fishing lures—as well as annotated suggestions about how to use all that equipment successfully—before we had left Sausalito. I figured, "Why not?" and gathered my wits, the fishing gear, and my willpower. By gosh, I was going to catch us a fish.

Following Chuck's advice, I trolled the lure out behind the boat from the special rack for the pole that I'd installed in the after port side of the boat. I didn't really expect anything to happen, but there was a strike almost immediately! I heard the reel shrieking and buzzing as the line played out before I really knew what was happening, and it took me a few moments to realize that I should go over and grab the pole. I was yelling, "Ann, I got a fish! I got a fish! Come on deck, it's a big one!"

She got there just in time to see the pole give a downward lurch in my hands and then just stay there, limp in my hands. Nothing. I drew in the line to find that there was nothing at all on the other end. No hook, no leader, no sinker, no lure. Nothing. The 50-pound test line had snapped. "There! See?" I said triumphantly to Ann. "Everybody says that fishing on the open sea is impossible. No need even to try it!" Surely, I thought, I wouldn't have to try this again. I put away the fishing gear.

Three times during the voyage, I tried the same thing. And three times, it was a failure. The second and third times, I heard the reel shriek as it did the first time; I grabbed the rod, I tightened the arresting brake, and I started reeling in the line. Again, a snap, and there was no more fish or gear on the end of the line. Obviously, I knew little about fishing (and didn't really want to) for surely I could have played the line and had a better chance of bringing in whatever fish that had had the good fortune to hook itself up with *my* fishing.

Both times, I told Ann with as much authority as I could muster that the fish I'd caught were so enormous that it was hopeless to try to get it onto the boat with nothing more than a 50-pound test line. Both times, I assured her I wasn't giving up but merely using common sense and waiting until we got into waters where the fish were smaller. Ann knew the real reason: I hated to fish.

Within four miles of the breakwater that announces arrival into Ensenada, we were in a calm. We'd been in two days of calm and one day of excellent wind and were eager to anchor in our first Mexican port. As we lazily inched forward in the slight breeze, a large-powered fishing dory came close; it carried several Mexican fishermen. I could see that they had a fresh catch of fish, so I waved to them to come alongside. I called out, *"Se vende pescado?"* thinking—hoping, rather, since I do not speak Spanish—that it means, "Do you sell fish?"

It must have meant that or something close, because they came alongside, turned off the motor, and held out a three-foot long codfish. I asked, in my most careful phrase-book Spanish, "Cuanto dinero?"

The Mexican skipper answered, "Speak English, please. It's two dollars."

I swallowed twice and said we'd take it if they'd give us a tow into the harbor because we had no engine. They all raised their black eyebrows in surprise and rapidly spoke among themselves. I assumed they were remarking about this crazy gringo who had come sailing down to Mexico without an engine, but the skipper answered back, "Okay, but we got no gas."

Fortunately, I had about three gallons in a can right at my

feet, so I gave it and two dollars to the skipper. They gave us the fish, took our bowline and towed us into a safe anchorage in Ensenada harbor next to a number of fine-looking yachts.

We'd finally arrived in Mexico. Our Trip was not only underway, it had reached a milestone. We'd sailed to one of the places we'd dreamed of getting to. Ann and I were proud of ourselves for making the voyage so far, from San Francisco to Ensenada, Mexico, with no working engine . . . on an untried, lateen-rigged sailing vessel . . . against the advice and sneers from friends and acquaintances. And now we *knew* beyond a doubt that this boat could sail anywhere. I think the *Felucca* was proud, too.

Now here we were, almost two months away from any contact with any other human being, not Bill, not another skipper, not a shopkeeper or soldier or sailor, and we didn't miss any of them. Don't get me wrong: Bill is a charming, delightful person, as are so very many of the wonderful people we've met and have come to love dearly. And we've thoroughly enjoyed the company of almost everyone we've ever met. Neither of us begrudges anyone for anything, and we both talked about how fortunate we were to have so many friends. I believed that then, and I believe it now. It's just that we discovered, out there in the middle of the vast Pacific, that our solitude is one of our most highly prized possessions. In solitude, we found the best of all possible discoveries: ourselves.

July 21—Pygmalion, change your health

Looking back at the way I was when I started sailing for a living—and I mean those words; I mean finding that the way to live is to sail—I find some key changes that I made in how I lived that have proved fundamental to the wonderful way things are now. I believe now that I could take any normal, healthy employed person who is overweight, distraught with personal problems, and disenchanted with the world as it is, and work with that person in a Pygmalion-like fashion. I'd get that person to do what I've done. "I did these things," I'll say, "and if you do them too, you'll be as healthy as you've ever been." After six to eight months of this work in an easy-to-follow and enjoyable routine,

144

I firmly believe that s/he would become a new person. These seven suggestions would be at the basis of our work:

1. Row everyday. Rowing is better exercise than walking, bicycling, or jogging. This single vigorous exercise will keep arms, torso, and lower body in excellent physical condition.

2. Change your eating habits for the better. Most people consume too much of the wrong foods every single day, mistakenly believing those foods to be necessary for their health. Never overindulge.

3. Change your drinking habits. Avoid hard liquors, caffeine beverages, and anything with sugar or synthetics. If alcohol is included, confine it to dry wines and champagnes only. Never, never overindulge. Don't drink alcohol at all is the best advice.

4. Avoid nicotine in all forms. If smoking is unavoidable, use something sweet (perhaps peppermint tea or something else that's sweet and natural . . .).

5. Sail. Cruise. Travel without a schedule to maintain. At first, perhaps a short (four weeks?) period of travel without a schedule might be all that a person can manage; a life without a schedule imposed from outside a person's own choices is the goal. Cruising will get you away from that television set (throw it away!).

6. Continue cruising and traveling. In every port can be found *something* to do if some extra cash is needed. Cash isn't the goal; cruising and traveling is. There's no room for a rocking chair on a sailboat; rocking chairs are seductive liars in that even as you're moving you're getting nowhere.

7. Take a companion, someone you love—friend, lover, relative, it doesn't matter so long as the two of you like, respect, and understand enough about each other so that you can take pleasure in sharing your discoveries with each other.

8. Don't cheat. Take each experience for what it really, really is. Don't let yourself imagine that it's something it really isn't. Don't "judge" it by thinking it's "good" or "bad." Just experience it. Try to learn something from it without belittling it or making it into something more significant than what it was at the time.

145

9. Keep on rowing, no matter what.

After a few months of following these suggestions, any person will find physical and emotional improvements. With continuing efforts along the lines of these suggestions, this newfound youth will remain with that person throughout a normal lifetime and then some. That's why I sometimes call Paradise "the fountain of youth." If you do those things, you'll most certainly get older, just like anybody else. *But you won't get old!!* You won't have to worry about "providing for your old-age" if you never get old. Besides, in Paradise, nobody's *old*, no matter how many years they've accumulated in terms of calendar records!

July 22—World record

The sky cleared for the first time in a month and I finally got a good noon sight. Since we haven't stood a wheel watch during the voyage, I'm less awestruck by Joshua Slocum's story of how he sailed two thousand miles across an ocean with his *Spray* steering herself. The *Frisco Felucca II* has done it three thousand miles; if she continues all the way, she'll add it up to 3,400 miles of self-steering across the Pacific, from Mexico to Hawaii!!

I don't really know exactly what's the reason why this boat constantly self-steers. Shape of the hull? Sail balance? Lateen rig? Some combination of many factors? I'll let the expert sailing engineers figure out the specific details. Whatever the reason is, I'm thankful. If we had had to steer this entire way, exhaustion and boredom would have consumed both of us and ruined the days of pleasure we've had. As it is, Ann and I are well-rested, in good health, and looking forward to seeing Hawaii.

About the only thing I'd do differently when we leave Hawaii is arrange to have more food on board somehow. Fish is fine and healthy, but nothing but fish is like nothing but anything else: it gets old. We make up games about how we're really eating something else, but those games don't really work.

July 23—Captain Nemo? Lights

Bursts of light, several at a time, flash eerily from well beneath the surface of the ocean at night. We've been observing these strange, slightly scary sights for the past two weeks about a thousand miles east of Hawaii. When I first saw them, I couldn't imagine what they were . . . flashes from Captain Nemo's submarine? Well, that was as good an explanation as anything *else*! They look like automobile headlights that are being rapidly turned on and off where each flash lasts about two seconds at the most. Each flash comes from below the surface and is so bright that it is startling . . . then another one . . . then another one . . . one here . . . one there . . . a few seconds apart, a few feet to thirty yards from the boat. Ann and I have finally decided that they are caused by dolphins. Their rapid movements create explosions of phosphoresence that halo their bodies and their lightning-like movements cause flashes like searchlights under water. We're not certain, though.

We marvel over the continuing magnificence and mystery of the sea.

July 24

The sun has been peeking in and out of the clouds all day, so my noon sight is unreliable once again. The sun is south of us instead of north as previously, and I don't know whether to add or subtract the declination. If we miss the Hawaiian Islands we'll be in real trouble. This fish diet can't last forever, and we have but four or five gallons of water left. The fresh fish help by providing some water, and my seawater rations help, too. Sometimes I wash down the seawater with a freshwater chaser, but that can't last much longer. Ann's beginning to watch the water supply more closely than ever before, and I know she's worried, too.

We have plenty of seasonings and oil to prepare fish practically any way, and we still have enough kerosene to use for fuel and light. Funny, though, how the thought of not surviving doesn't seem like a major concern anymore. We've survived this far, and so long as we keep our wits about us we'll survive for a long time yet.

The weather had been cloudy—and frequently stormy—for the past month, so I haven't been able to take Polaris for the true latitude I desperately need. This morning I added the mizzen sail beneath the mainsail, positioned low on the same mast. We're making good speed with all sails in the 18 mph breeze. I've found eight specific, different ways to set our sails, depending on the force and direction of the wind, in such a way so that the *Felucca* continues to steer herself.

There are small brown fish hiding inside our wells, and they've eaten off the barnacles that grew there in Puerto Vallarta.

We've been at sea fifty-five days and our eagerness to get to Hawaii crops up increasingly in a moment of anxiety. I wasn't aware that our landfall had become that important until Ann remarked today that we might have spaghetti and meatballs for dinner tonight. We don't *have* spaghetti or meatballs! Just the mention of food other than fish sets our mouths watering, and Ann has trouble keeping her mind off foods other than fish!

I've come to believe that everyone who makes a transoceanic voyage such as this one ought to take plenty of "refreshment," some kind of relaxant. Ours is wine and chess and cards. Every afternoon or early evening, Ann and I relax with a glass or two of wine over a game of chess or gin. Sir Francis Chichester took several kinds of liquor and beer in "ample quantities" on this around-the-world single-handed voyage and said the same sort of thing. Now I understand why I agree so wholeheartedly. If a sailor can have his favorite form of "grog," once a day in reasonably small doses, s/he stands a much greater chance of remaining relaxed during the crossing. And I *don't* mean that I'm endorsing overindulgence in anything; any good sailor always needs his wits about him!

July 25—Closing in on Hilo

My last questionable sight was latitude 21 degrees, 21 minutes, so we must head south to be right on latitude 19 degrees, 50 minutes for Hilo. In this cloudy weather it's absolutely necessary to be on the correct latitude; we don't want to bypass Hawaii!! I change tack often these days and am continually adjusting the sails. This seems almost an imposition because, overall, our crossing has been so simple! I realize my busyness is probably due to our/my increased nervousness as our voyage is nearing its end. After all, a first landfall after such a long first ocean voyage on such a small boat ought to get anyone excited and nervous, oughtn't it?

Noon brought sunshine and clear skies. Eureka! I got a clear sun sight, putting us at 21 degrees latitude and 152.1 longitude—very close to the mark needed for Hilo. Mid-afternoon my mouth fell open and I thought my eyes played tricks on me; the long ice vapor steam of a jet airplane appeared in the sky, paralleling our southwest course! I yelled to Ann to come take a look. Civilization! We've not seen any evidence of other people's presence on this planet for a long time. Fifteen minutes later I saw another white vapor stream and the jet itself going in the opposite direction. That confirms that we're "close" to Hawaii. Ann and I were relieved and giggling, congratulating ourselves that we're this close to our exotic 50th state.

Early evening now. Clouds have returned. Ann is sitting on deck scanning the horizon back and forth, round and round, looking for land. I can't get her to come below. This is a real reverse for her. During these entire two years on board together, she's spent only a few minutes a day on deck when it's been this cloudy. A few minutes ago, I kidded her about it. She laughed, but she didn't want to stop. Then she called down to me to come and see a tanker on the horizon. Yes, there was a tanker on the horizon, about eight miles away, heading in our direction. As we watched, the ship changed course and moved away from us. That's odd. Why would she suddenly turn, so far out from land and well into her shipping lane? Ann and I decided that they were coming close to see if we needed assistance; when they got within binocular range and saw we were steering for land under full sail, they must have been satisfied we were doing fine. So they turned back to their original course. I couldn't observe them by glass because I hadn't replaced my long "Captain Kidd" telescope that was stolen in Puerto Vallarta.

The trade winds have petered out, but we're still in a good mood. Ann came down and served us up two cocktails of rice tea. We enjoyed grilled fish and pretended it was *filet mignon*. Progress until now, bedtime, has been slow in light air and intermittent showers.

We're not down and out by any means, but we're not in our usual good spirits. It's time to take a break. Time to anchor somewhere. We're going to make it, though. For sure. The sea has taken so many people, so many unfortunate sailors. It's not going to take us.

Later—What happened to David?

I keep thinking of David Brooks. How many times on this voyage have I gazed out over the wide Pacific and wondered, "Is this where Dave's boat capsized?" "Did Dave die near this place?" He was more than merely a competent sailor—he was an outstanding sailor. What happened to him? I've gone over the circumstances that surrounded his disappearance and I still don't understand. The Coast Guard had reported that Dave's red trimaran was found about 140 miles off the coast of San Francisco, floating upside down but almost totally intact. How long could he and Bob go on their eight-foot rubber lifeboat on the high seas? How long could they stay alive with scant provisions and navigating equipment? Surely the Pacific took David, but how?

David was too good a sailor simply to have fallen overboard and drowned, no matter what the weather or the boat's problem. One evening when I was visiting him at Lou's house, I heard him tell a friend why he sailed the way he did. The friend asked, "How come you live such a life, David, taking big chances, sailing your beautiful trimaran at top speed in rough oceans when you know you're balancing on the edge of the abyss?"

David answered, "That's where it really is for me. I must drink in all the satisfaction I get from balancing on the edge. The risk is the game. I'd hate to have life pass me by because I didn't have guts enough to take chances. You know, the yacht clubs and piers of the world are full of would-be sailors who could never shove away from the dock. Even though I do take some chances, I've become pretty adept at handling my boat. For me, the greatest feeling in the world is the freedom and exhilaration of taking *Far Horizons* across oceans using only the wind for propulsion, tying down the helm to the self-steering device and letting her bound as fast as she can sail!"

One morning before David and his nephew, Bob, were to leave for Costa Rica—the same day Ann and I were to leave for Mexico on *Our Trip*—he asked Ann and me to join him and a few other friends in sailing the *Far Horizons* for a while. That boat was an unbelievable sailing machine. There was a light wind blowing about twelve miles per hour when David eased her downwind out of our small harbor into what I remarked was a "lazy sailing wind."

Dave responded, "Lazy? In that case, I'll make my own wind." He took the wheel from Ann and came around into the wind. Our speed tripled with a sudden lurch! It was amazing to me, a dyed-in-the-wool single-hull sailor for more than twenty-five years at that time, to experience such swift and speedy response of a vessel in such little wind. We were almost flying! Dave played a tape for us on his tape recorder, made during one of his previous crossings to the Hawaiian Islands. His voice on the tape said the *Far Horizons* was moving at 27 mph, that they were in 35 to 40 mph winds about a thousand miles out from San Francisco. There was a singing, high-pitched sound, an eerie steady scream of wind. We could hear the sound of water pounding on the hull and an intermittent, high metallic shriek, which David explained was made by the vibrations of the steel centerboard. We heard his voice occasionally, shouting comments like, "Wow! . . . I don't believe it! . . . Far out! . . ." And we heard the whoosh of the spray that streamed past the lower pontoon.

After listening to the tape, I remarked, "David, you're a real speed freak, aren't you?"

"Yes, I guess I am . . . I have a hard time keeping crew members, especially girls. Usually after one crossing, they head for shore and I never see them again." He wasn't bragging. He sounded like he was just stating a simple fact.

I said, "I'm not used to this kind of speed on a boat and, frankly, it scares me." We didn't even have all the sails up, and I didn't even want to imagine how it would be with all sails in place in a fresh gale aboard the *Far Horizons*. I remember, though, how David answered my comments about being afraid of the kind of speed that he thrived on.

"T. Jay, this is what it's all about for me. Now, *you* are one of the loosest sailors I've ever met! I wouldn't do what you are about to do, so we're even! You're going to Mexico with a $15 sextant, a pocket compass, a Bulova wristwatch, no engine, no radio, and a AAA roadmap! You could get *lost* out there!" David and I just laughed.

The next day was the day Ann and I left at dawn for Mexico.

David left a little later and overtook us about fifteen miles out from San Francisco. Even in the light wind, the *Far Horizons* came from far behind us and overtook us with startling speed, moving like a strange but proud red swan under way.

Dave shouted to us as they got close, "Hey, Cap'n! You want me to tow you out further for a better offing?"

"Sure," I shouted back.

"Hold on," he yelled as he tossed us the line. "It'll be a hard tug!"

It was a hard tug, indeed. The slack came out of that line like a whip, the nylon's stretching as if it were about to snap. I was awed by the force of the tremendous pull. Trimarans don't push through the water but stay on top, converting almost every ounce of the wind's energy into speed and power, and David's *Far Horizons* was skimming over the water like a power skater as she tugged us effortlessly along. He towed us for a while and then I tossed his towline free. I took final photographs of David and his beloved vessel as they circled the *Felucca* for a fine farewell.

We had a happy visit in Puerto Vallarta weeks later. David was a good friend. He left Mexico for Hawaii via Costa Rica a few days before we did, and we vowed to meet someday in Hilo.

We never saw him again after that last meeting in Puerto Vallarta.

July 26—Frenzy fishing again

I got another sun sight. The wind has shifted to the east. Ann asked me to catch more fish, so I did. About 6:00 p.m. the wind jumped suddenly to force five, but the sea stayed smooth and calm. The *Felucca* took off with a lurch, like a frightened hippo. The stronger the wind the better she sails, and in the flat sea we seem to be flying well above the water's surface!

July 27—Rudder "loose" again

It's cloudy . . . no sun sight today . . . rained off and on all day and tonight. My dead reckoning puts us within 19.50 latitude

David Brooks

and 153 longitude. The wind is down to force four as we continue to move westward.

Water is gone. I'm still drinking seawater daily, but Ann refuses. She says she'll get enough water by eating fish and that we'll be on land before she has any real problem. We both are feeling restless—tonight Ann had a brief bout with an illness feeling—and both of us have "the trots." I don't think it's the seawater, because Ann hasn't drunk any at all. Maybe it's metabolic rebellion against fish. Or anticipation that's gone on too long.

The rudder is coming loose again, but I'm telling it to stay in one piece just a few more days. I don't want to go into the water to fix it again.

Ann keeps my moustache trimmed. Since it got long enough to look like it was planned, my cornet lip is the best ever. So, cup instrument players: improve your playing and grow a moustache. It forces me to lower the mouthpiece on my lips, giving me a bigger range. That position makes the difference between good and excellent playing. I remember the first time I saw Louis Armstrong play; he had a scarred upper lip because he used only a small amount of it to reach high C and F above high C so frequently (and so beautifully). Growing this moustache has forced me to place the mouthpiece correctly; after all these years of playing, this is a phenomenal discovery for me.

Ann's asleep. I'm planning what I'll wear when we go ashore. None of my clothes fits anymore. My waist went from 34 to 28 since we left California. The last of my baby fat is finally gone, and my muscles are well-tuned and hard. I've decided to wear my blue captain's hat, turtleneck tee shirt, and blue trousers. I'll wear that tooled leather belt with its pounded silver buckle of an Arabian horse's head. And I'll polish those Mexican sandals to a patent-leather shine and wear them, too. Ann plans to sew a vest from a tanned deer hide—from my last three-point buck—she never has any problems with clothes. She designs and makes her own. Her weight and proportions haven't changed significantly since she was sixteen years old. She has made some beautiful long Hawaiian-type print dresses and pants; she'll be a knockout, though, in anything she chooses.

Clouds hit Polaris this evening. We're lost.

No, we're semi-lost. I'm going to head south to latitude 18, then crisscross back to 20 degrees, continuing to the west. The Hawaiian Islands cover enough of an area that we should see something before too much longer. If the weather were clear, I could hone right in on our destination.

I got a hard case of wishful thinking and turned on the little AM-FM radio. My daughter, Sean, gave it to me to use as a direction finder. It worked! And I heard two Hilo radio stations! I guess my letting the batteries sit unused most of the way let this happen, but I had thought they were dead. The radio stations correspond with my dead reckoning so I feel reassured about our position.

July 28—Hilo light

Ann's on deck again, ignoring the clouds and searching for land. We're both on edge today. I'm continually adjusting the sails just to be having something to do. Ann looks for land. Our routine has changed rather abruptly in the past twenty-four hours and the only reason for it seems to be our impatience now to get to Hawaii.

There are no jet vapor trails from the planes today. Or at least there doesn't seem to be any up there when the clouds break enough to let me see through to the open sky. There are unusual numbers of birds flying near the boat, successfully hunting fish whether they're flying or swimming. The clouds are darkest over where Hilo ought to be.

The plastic sextant, hand compass, and portable radio are not sufficient as navigational aids. I'm going to get full nautical tables so that I can take sights of the sun, stars, and planets at any opportunity. I did get a Polaris sight a while ago, and it puts us at 19.10 degrees, about forty miles northwest of Hilo. I changed tack and put the course halfway between that earlier radio fix and the star fix.

Because of the lengthy duration of the trip, our food and water problems, and the recent combination of our edginess and closeness of our destination, I didn't sleep well last night and am writing this about midnight, on deck, with lantern. I was sitting here, in my sawed-off captain's chair, and was jolted by the awareness in the corner of my eye of what I thought instantly was

155

lightning on the horizon about where those clouds were over Hilo earlier. I saw nothing more when I looked. I squeezed my eyes tightly shut for a few moments to increase my night vision and then riveted my eyes over the starboard bow to look for another flash. There it was! I knew it was real!

I rushed below and looked carefully at the chart. It had to be the Hilo light! I was so excited that I almost woke Ann, but decided to time the flash and maybe wake her later. If the flashes came at ten-minute intervals, it would definitely be the Hilo light. Well, sure enough, it flashed its short burst of several flashes ten minutes later. It was the greatest emotional ejaculation I'd ever had. The greatest, the most unbeatable, the ultimate. Selfishly, I gloried in it alone. After all, we'd made it to Hawaii! I decided to let Ann sleep and wake in the morning to the wonderful surprise of her own discovery; by then we'd be where she could see the land she'd been searching for these last few days!

I woke her at dawn with a cup of coffee and asked her to skip making breakfast (I told her I didn't want to eat any fish just yet and would she please just go on deck for a while). She went up, screamed with delight, and called me up to come and see. It was her (and my) first sight of land in well over two months. It was beautiful. We gulped in the view of the green sugarcane fields, little specks of beach "houses and smoke from Moa Nui volcano. Ann collapsed! We were so giddy with excitement that I thought this was a peculiar joke of some kind, but I quickly realized that she had fainted!

I didn't know what to do! She didn't answer my frantic calls to her, and I was holding her head closely to mine. Finally, her eyes fluttered, she regained consciousness, and I helped her sit groggily upright. I comforted her the best I could. My thoughts were racing: Gawd, what would I do without her?

I think our unbalanced diet and lack of water had just made her weak. I didn't feel weak at all, but I had been drinking seawater regularly—never more than two cups at the most in one day, however—and she had not drunk any at all; she hadn't had any freshwater in several days and had relied on the fresh fish to give her the water her body needed.

July 29—Made it

This morning at 6:30, we could see the island of Hawaii clearly. Mauna Kea and Mauna Loa were hidden in the clouds. Our diet of saltwater and fish was over.

On course for Hilo. Wind dropped from force six to force two. The clouds dispersed a bit later in the day, and the island was clearly visible all afternoon and tonight. We've seen distant smokestacks and the lower parts of two volcanoes. We don't want to enter the strange harbor in the black of this night, so we've hove to and plan to sail in at dawn.

July 30—Last scare before dropping

Wouldn't you know it! The last three miles have been the most dangerous we've had in many days! Before dawn the wind rose to force five. We wanted to go on in, however, and we didn't hesitate. At daylight we were approaching port with all working sails full. I hoisted the stars and stripes and my Corinthian Club banner. I hoped the wind would subside so that I could enter the harbor easily, but it didn't. It quickly rose to force six.

We'd been so excited at arriving safely that we were too nonchalant about the breakers. We had drifted closer to the beach than we should have as we entered through the Hilo breakwater. I had put us into that proverbial painted corner. We were being buffeted by 35 mph steady winds and large breakers just before the entrance, so we had to sail broadside to the combers as we entered. Each wave slammed us broadside and brutally slammed the vessel sideways. I'd put up all working sails in order to make a good showing, but we were hardly making the trimphant entry I'd planned. I had too much sail for the strength of the wind, I knew, but this was our last gasp, and I'd figured why not?

As we got closer, it became clear why not. There was no going back and no way to get another try at entering. We either would make it on our first try or be driven ashore by the crashing breakers and smashed on the rocky-strewn beach. Two large sailing yachts had gotten curious about our boat and approached us twice. We raced on, not daring to slow down or change course, and the seas slammed us continually; all sails were straining, all pennants and flags were stiff in the wind. We missed crashing at the entrance by not more than three feet. But we made it!

Even with no rudder much of the way, the *Felucca* steered herself the entire voyage, all the way from Puerto Vallarta to Hilo!!! This must be a world's record! I should register it with somebody.

After 3,400 miles in sixty-three days and ten hours, we dropped our anchor at 10:00 a.m. near the sandy beach at Hilo's entrance harbor. And just at the moment the anchor dug in and the *Felucca* began her rounding up to the wind, the topping lift parted! This lift holds the large mainsail to the top of the mast, so the heavy yard and sail came slamming down to the deck. I heard it split and shouted to Ann to jump clear. It missed us both. And I figured, what the heck! We're *anchored*, for Pete's sake! We don't *need* that sail right now! We see the town of Hilo; the air is heavy with the scents of tropical flowers and wet leaves, and there are emeralds of greenery everywhere we look. We took much longer to make the crossing than we'd thought we would, but we made it. We're here now, and it's time to explore Hawaii. That topping lift can wait!

Later—Paradise is now

We made it not only to Hawaii. We had found a place far, far better. When Ann and I started out, we both looked at Hawaii as a "Paradise" we'd reach when we got there. At some point, however, we discovered that we actually *lived* in Paradise. We'd already entered it and didn't even know it. We were pleasantly surprised that first day, anchored at Hilo, to realize that Hawaii is simply one of the many glorious places right in our own backyard! Sausalito is my home port, my boat is my home, and the water is my yard, gardens, and special treasure chest. I live in Paradise, indeed.

In Paradise, I became healthier than I've ever been. Today I'm younger than ever. After all, there's only one Ann, only one me, and only this moment to live. There are simply too many things to enjoy in each living moment to worry about what might happen. Or to be afraid of things over which I have no power. In

Paradise, even the fear of dying has a way of just withering away. When that happens, the fear of living leaves too. It was out there, in the profound silence of the sea, that I began to understand what Paradise actually is for me. It's dreaming about things and seeing dream after dream actually come true! It's not having any money worries even when the money's all gone. It's blowing a tune on my cornet when I feel happy. It's welcoming each sunrise with a gratitude that bursts out without even *trying* to feel it. It's being afraid of things that can genuinely hurt you, but not so afraid that I can't figure out how to deal with them. It's not being afraid of things that cannot genuinely hurt you. It's being not afraid of other people, being not afraid of not having any money. It's the ability to haul up the anchor and sail off into the sunrise on any day that seems somehow special in its own way. It's in being able to look and actually *see* the rainbows that are really out there. It's being able sometimes even to *touch* a rainbow. Paradise is in each moment, in tasting everything each moment offers and savoring it to the fullest. It's all that. And more. Life in Paradise has had its quiet way in rearranging basic priorities to where even some major disasters have led to adventures and rewards even more wonderful than the last ones.

The *Felucca* was taken from us in Hawaii. It was a terrible thing. It was stolen from us, right under our eyes. While it was being towed, things went wrong and the sea took her. She smashed to pieces in the pounding surf and jagged rocks. We lost her and everything on her. She met a spectacular end. It was a sad and shocking thing to watch.

I know that if I'd lost her earlier during any of those near-misses we had had during the voyage to Hawaii I would have probably lost my self as well. During the first part of the voyage, even *thinking* the *Felucca* was near the end was enough to send me into deep depression and despair. Sad to say, but early on in our voyage my boat was more precious to me in many ways than even my beloved Ann. That particular priority simply disappeared in Paradise.

Yes, I got very angry over the *Felucca II's* destruction, but I was surprised to discover that I wasn't destroyed by any means. After a few months in Hawaii, we borrowed some money and went back home to Sausalito. Not too long after that, Ann and I spent a few years investigating and exploring more of our huge backyard. We took two and a half years and went around the world. There have been many voyages since then, as Paradise has become more real and tangible, more and more frequently. Of course, there's a *Felucca III*. And today there's even a *Frisco Felucca IV*.

And all that is truly another story.

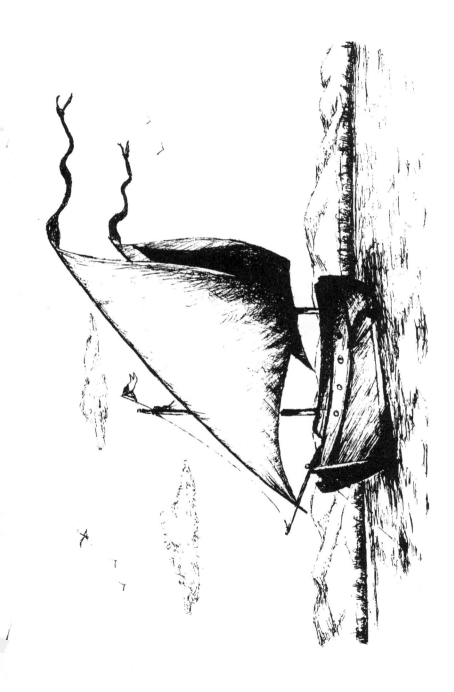